Dr. Jennifer Londgren

A GUIDE TO

MENTAL
&
EMOTIONAL
WELLNESS

Biblical wisdom
Practical principles
Clinical insight

D1496190

Published by Straight Talk Books
P.O. Box 301, Milwaukee, WI 53201
800.661.3311 · timeofgrace.org

Printed in the United States of America
ISBN: 978-1-949488-78-4

CONTENTS

PREFACE

It can be overwhelming to watch the news or a Facebook news feed and see what people are talking about. It's disappointing and alarming to read the headlines and see what is happening in our country. Wars, rumors of war, drug overdoses, murders, diseases, and not only the acceptance but the promotion of things that are clearly against the Bible. The world is struggling. And along with it, our mental health is struggling, and depression and anxiety rates have skyrocketed. Suicidal thoughts are occurring now in children as young as first grade. Drug use and self-medication have increased and pose a grave danger because of drugs such as fentanyl that are fatal even with a small consumption.

As a Christian, it is easy to become overwhelmed with the way people treat each other. What type of world do we have to leave for our children and grandchildren? It's hard to know what is best and how to navigate these modern challenges. As we explore these modern issues, we can rest assured that we have a timeless solution. God is with us, and God is for us. God hears us when we cry out to him, and he answers our prayers. The world has struggled before, and it will continue to struggle, but on our side we have the God who created the world by speaking. He created all of us and sent his only Son to die for us.

This is the God who knows you personally. He knows every challenging thought you have, the mental health issues or addictions that you or someone you love struggles with, and the difficult and painful feelings that you experience.

We make an impact on others when we serve them out of Christ's love for us. In Matthew 5:13 Jesus said, **"You are the salt of the earth. But if the salt loses its saltiness, how can it be made salty again? It is no longer good for anything, except to be thrown out and trampled underfoot."** This is a critically important passage for Christians. In Jesus' time, salt was extremely valuable because it was so rare. Jesus was saying that Christians are precious and add seasoning to the world. But sometimes as we become burdened with the stressors and hopelessness of the world, we feel ourselves losing our zest for life and falling into despair.

Jesus also said, **"You are the light of the world,"** and, **"In the same way, let your light shine before others, that they may see your good deeds and glorify your Father in heaven"** (Matthew 5:14,16). You hear phrases like "let your light shine," but what happens when you feel like the only light shining in the darkness and that your light doesn't feel powerful enough to illuminate the space around you? What happens when you feel your light dimming? What if you want to let your light shine but feel darkness creeping inside of you. How do you ensure that your light stays bright? The power of our lights shining comes through Christ alone, and this book will outline other ways, along with God's Word, to keep your light shining brightly as you navigate your everyday life. The world needs the light of Christians and the hope of Jesus now more than ever. My prayer is that you will find this book to be encouraging and supportive and that it will help ignite a flame in you to become the best version of yourself—the version God created you to become.

Along with his Word, God gives us knowledge and tools that we can utilize to cope with our mental health. The purpose of this book is to bring together Bible wisdom and principles of wellness and support them with modern psychological principles and self-care and wellness strategies. I will include questions you can use to process the information more deeply and journaling prompts that you can complete on your own. My hope and prayer is that you can optimize your own health—spiritual, emotional, physical, and relational—and be able to support those in your life to your full capacity.

As the world and the people in it are struggling so deeply, I believe that as Christians it is our time to let the light of Christ shine. It is our time to support our neighbors and serve our communities with the biblical principles of peace, love, and generosity. In order to do this, we ourselves must be physically, emotionally, and spiritually well. The goal of this book is to help you optimize your mental health and spiritual wellness. I believe that when Christians are mentally and emotionally healthier, their marriages are stronger, their kids feel safer, the communities they serve flourish, and the church thrives.

CHAPTER 1
OVERVIEW

I'll never forget the moment I made the decision to start taking better care of myself. It was August 2019. It was the most important year of my position as a tenure track faculty at Minnesota State University, Mankato. I was also working as a mental health therapist with a caseload of clients. At that particular time, I was anticipating returning to teaching full time at the end of the month, after being on maternity leave following the birth of my third baby. I sat in my living room and felt an overwhelming sense of anxiety and panic. I felt dread. How was I going to manage this? I had a five-year-old, three-year-old, and a six-month-old, all who stayed at home. How could I do this? How could I be a wife, a mom, a professor, and a mental health therapist all at once? How could I serve those under my care with my whole self when I was stretched so thin? I felt like I was drowning. The harder I was struggling to get air, the faster I was sinking. I prayed to God in that moment to help me. I prayed for guidance and wisdom as I navigated my vocations.

In that moment, I knew I had two options. One option was to do less. The issue was that doing less didn't feel like an option to me. At home I wanted to be a fully present and engaged mother to my young children. I wanted to be a supportive and encouraging wife to my husband. Professionally, I taught in a program that trained students to become counselors for people with addiction, a job that I consider to be lifesaving work. As a therapist, I worked with clients who struggled with mental health challenges. I cared deeply about their well-being and knew that stopping my work with them wasn't an option either. I realized I didn't want to live in survival mode, plagued by guilt and frustration and a constant feeling of missing out or not doing a good enough job. Living like that wasn't an option for me. I knew that there had to be a way where I could not just survive but really thrive as I navigated my journey as a working mom.

Doing less wasn't an option, so taking care of myself better became my only choice. Optimizing my sleep, my time, my relationships and support system, and my mental and emotional health was my route to getting out of survival mode and serving in my vocations to my fullest. That afternoon in August was a turning point for me. I continued praying. I started reading. I started listening to podcasts. I started sitting quietly and noticing my thought patterns. I started practicing gratitude. I started studying my emotions and sharing them. I started being intentional with my physical health. I began connecting with people with whom I wanted to deepen my relationships.

As I practiced these strategies, I saw them beginning to work. My anxiety became manageable. I started to feel joy and excitement, and I started talking about what I was doing for my mental and emotional health. In October 2019, I decided that I would like to teach other professionals all these strategies of self-care. I also started teaching my students strategies of self-care and in some classes began every class period by presenting a strategy and having my students discuss and practice it. I developed a training based on the personal work I was doing and entitled it, "Deconstructing Self-Care: Helping Professionals Thrive in a Weary World."

I was set to present at a conference that was taking place in April 2020 when the world shut down because of a global pandemic. The conference was moved online. The number of attendees for that presentation was enormous because self-care and the weariness of the world had become a topic of interest like none other. Since that conference, I have been presenting on self-care, wellness, resiliency, mental health, crisis response, and anxiety for dozens of organizations and now thousands of people. It is my mission to share the strategies that are tried and true for me. These are not strategies that I have made up; they are from the Bible. God has outlined for us what we as Christians need to do to be mentally and emotionally well, and modern psychology has merely validated it.

The way I see it, my biggest job as a mom, second only to feeding the faith life of my children, is to take care of myself so I have the capacity to regulate my emotions and help them co-regulate theirs. Then every interaction, every response, every decision, and every conversation can be grounded in love, humor, joy, and wisdom instead of irritability, exhaustion, fear, and anger. If I can expand my own stress threshold and cope with the micro stress doses that life inevitably throws my way, I will help my kids develop the capacity not to eliminate stress in their lives but to process it and cope with it. It's my spiritual and ethical responsibility to take care of myself as a Christian because through Christ alone, I have a lot of work to do.

CHAPTER 2
WHAT IS SELF-CARE, AND WHY DOES IT MATTER?

"For we are God's handiwork, created in Christ Jesus to do good works, which God prepared in advance for us to do."
Ephesians 2:10

"Rest and self-care are so important. When you take time to replenish your spirit, it allows you to serve from the overflow. You cannot serve from an empty vessel."[1]
—Eleanor Brownn

I've talked with many people who say that they don't believe they deserve to practice self-care. To some, self-care is equated with selfishness. It's the antithesis of the life of a Christian, which is to live in service to God and your neighbor. It seems like it is the opposite of humbling yourself, of trusting in God, and in putting the needs of others above yourself. Self-care is associated with ex-travagance that might seem unnecessary, like getting massages or pedicures, or it might seem like something that might be nice to do *someday*. It becomes a *should* on our list of things to do, like minimizing our houses or meal planning or budgeting better. Even if some do attempt to engage in self-care, they do so feeling guilty or uneasy—because they could be doing something productive or spending more time with their kids. They may also feel guilty putting a burden of childcare or pet care on someone else in order to do the things they find nourishing for themselves. They might also have people in their lives who overtly tell them that what they are doing is selfish.

Oftentimes in marriages there is a dynamic where one spouse may be more likely to have fun and the other may be more practical. The more practical spouse may communicate frustration or instill a sense of guilt in the fun-loving partner: "We are parents; we can't go on a trip." "It's Saturday morning, we should be spending time with the kids, not golfing with friends." "You've gone hunting how many times this season?" The message tends to be: "I'm suffering, and you need to suffer too. I'm doing more than you, and you are being selfish by getting your needs met and not meeting mine."

We also might justify unproductive or excessive behavior by labeling it "self-care." Binge-watching a TV show until 2 A.M.? Self-care. Overspending on Amazon Prime? Self-care. Drinking three margaritas on a Friday night after work? Self-care.

I've asked my students what they do to engage in self-care, and they frequently give me answers related to their phones or social media. I remember one student saying, "I just get out my phone and watch TikTok videos for my self-care." If you've ever seen the show *Parks and Recreation*, there is an episode with a concept called "treat yo' self." In that particular show, two characters engage in excessive behavior like eating extravagant food, drinking fancy drinks, and spending a lot of money. As they do this, they say, "Treat yo' self!" My sister and I refer to this episode if we spend money on something impractical. "Just bought this thing: treat yo' self!"

Self-care isn't "treat yo' self." I'm not saying that you can never look at your phone, watch TV, have a drink or two, or buy yourself something fun. These are all normal behaviors that we do as a way of enjoying life. They aren't inherently wrong or sinful behaviors. The issues happen when these behaviors become coping strategies. When you feel bored, you look at your phone. When you feel empty or sad, you drink a few alcoholic beverages. When you feel antsy or anxious, you buy something to bring yourself relief. These behaviors may become a way to regulate your mood. This means that they provide a sense of relief when you feel discomfort or pain. Coping and regulating your emotions with these strategies is not self-care.

Self-care is defined by the World Health Organization as "the ability of individuals, families and communities to promote their own health, prevent disease, maintain health, and to cope with illness and disability with or without the support of a health worker."[2] Self-care includes everything related not only to staying physically healthy but also spiritually, emotionally, mentally, and socially healthy as well. A study published in *BMC Palliative Care* in April 2018 described self-care as being the "self-initiated behavior that people choose to incorporate to promote good health and general well-being."[3] Marni Amsellem, a licensed psychologist out of Trumbull, Connecticut, described self-care as "anything that you do for yourself that feels nourishing."[4] That definition strikes me because *nourishing* is defined as "containing substances necessary for growth, health, and good condition" by *Oxford Languages*.

The word *nourish* is found throughout the Bible. In the King James translation, it is found in Genesis 50:21. It's the story of Joseph. After his brothers had betrayed him and sold him into slavery, Joseph became a ruler of Egypt. Years later, when a famine struck Israel and Joseph's brothers came to Egypt looking for food, they realized the ruler was the brother whom they had betrayed. They were terrified that he would seek revenge. Instead of seeking revenge, however, Joseph forgave his brothers and comforted them saying, **"Therefore fear ye not: I will *nourish* you, and your little ones."** He was reassuring them that he would provide and take care of them. Just as Joseph promised to nourish his brothers and their offspring, God also nourishes us through his Word. When we do things that are nourishing for our faith, nourishing for our minds, nourishing for our bodies, and nourishing for our relationships, this is self-care.

WHY DOES IT MATTER THAT YOU TAKE CARE OF YOURSELF?

Sometimes in this self-care discussion, we focus on how we will take care of ourselves. We come up with lists of things that we can do that sound like they would be relaxing or fun. Instead of thinking about what we can do for self-care, let's start with *why* we should engage in self-care. The social commentator Simon Sinek has one of the most viewed TED Talks of all time entitled, "Start With Why." He gives examples of famous people throughout history who had a powerful *why*, like Martin Luther King Jr. or the Wright brothers. He discusses companies like Apple who lead their businesses with their *why* and how these individuals and companies are more successful and innovative when they have clarity in why they do what they do. He makes a case for leading with your mission and your purpose instead of with what you do and how you do it. Why do you do what you do? He says that Martin Luther King Jr. said, "I have a dream," not, "I have a plan."

The *what* and the *how* fall into place when you have a compelling *why*. So, I'm asking you: Why is it important that you take care of yourself and your health? Why does it matter if you, the salt of the earth, sustain your saltiness? Why does it matter if your light shines? Why does it matter if you are well?

Your *why* might be different than mine. To me, why I'm writing this book is that I want you to be healthy. I want you to be in heaven with me someday. I want you to have a deep sense of purpose and meaning and strong, connected relationships. I want your family members to feel safe and loved in your presence. I believe that if you as a Christian or someone interested in the faith are healthier, even by a little bit, then the church will thrive and the Word of God will spread. This is not by our doing but by the work of the Holy Spirit. The world needs the light of Christ's love; it needs the hope of eternal life; it needs the biblical truth; it needs saving. If we can be beacons of light in our fallen, broken world, then the darkness will fade. I'm here to help you let your light shine. If your light has felt dim lately or if you feel like you've lost it altogether, that's okay. You're not alone. This book is meant to help you find that light or brighten it.

REFLECTION BREAK

1. Write out why it matters that you take care of yourself:
   Spiritually:

Mentally:

Physically:

Socially:

2. Who needs you to be your best self?

WHAT ARE WAYS YOU CAN
TAKE CARE OF YOURSELF?

Once we have a compelling reason why it matters to take care of ourselves, let's examine some ways that we can engage in self-care. What are ways that we can nourish our bodies and minds? What are ways we can nourish our marriages and our close relationships? How do we view nourishing our bodies and minds as something necessary for us to do, and how do we do it motivated out of love instead of guilt, duty, shame, or fear? How do we associate nourishing our health and well-being with joy and love instead of feeling overwhelmed or like it's too much work? Take some time to reflect on the current self-care strategies that you currently use and that you would like to begin to implement:

Strategies I currently use to nourish my:

Spiritual health
Faith/soul:

Meaning/purpose:

Physical health
Body:

Mental health
Emotions:

Mind:

Social health

Marriage:

Relationships with family:

Relationships with friends:

Relationships with coworkers:

Our bodies and minds are intimately connected, and many strategies may be used to promote wellness in multiple areas. If I'm feeling worried or overwhelmed, I often pray to my heavenly Father. This is a strategy that promotes spiritual wellness, mental wellness, and physical wellness. I can feel my body relax as I talk to God, and I have a mental picture of myself literally casting my cares on him. We sometimes fragment our health or ourselves into separate pieces, but our bodies, souls, and minds are difficult to separate.

Another effective way to communicate safety to our bodies is to breathe deeply. Putting your hand on your heart is a way to communicate safety and compassion to yourself also. If you can pause and breathe deeply when you are triggered, this can have a profound impact on your relationships and how you handle conflict.

Now think of strategies that you would like to begin to implement. How would you like to improve your self-care in these areas? Remember, this isn't just done by us alone. Pray to God to grant you wisdom as you discern useful strategies. Pray to God that his will be done in your life. Pray for his help. Talk with your loved ones about how you would like to improve and what they need from you to feel supported.

Be specific; be as creative as you can! Think of how you would genuinely like to cultivate health in these areas. Don't just list what you think the "right" answer is.

How would you, as a unique child of God,
like to improve your self-care in these areas?

Spiritual health

Faith/soul:

Meaning/purpose:

Physical health

Body:

Mental health

Emotions:

Mind:

Social health

Marriage:

Relationships:

SELF-TALK

A few years ago, there was a trending YouTube video of Jessica's daily affirmations. If you have no idea what I'm talking about, do yourself a favor and go check it out. It's a video of a little blond girl in her pajamas standing on her bathroom counter and talking to herself in the mirror. She goes through a list of stuff that she likes with great enthusiasm and vigor. She happily calls out things like: "I like my stuff. I like my dad. I like my hair. I like my haircuts. My whole house is great. I can do anything good." This video is so adorable and uplifting. It feels good to see a child basking in the joy of who she is and confident in herself.

The way we communicate to ourselves is one of our most critical forms of communication. How many times do we criticize ourselves, insult ourselves, taunt ourselves inside our own minds? How many times is the voice in our heads sarcastic, exasperated, overwhelmed, or downright abusive? With many of the clients I work with, I'm shocked to hear the things they report saying to themselves: "You deserve to feel this way." "You are struggling, and that's not okay. It's your fault." "Everyone would be better off if you were dead."

When our self-talk is cruel and abusive, it takes away our joy, our energy, and our confidence. We would never say to a friend the things we say to ourselves, and we would never hang out with a friend who says the things to us that we say to ourselves. One thing that I have noticed in my work with specifically Christian clients is that I think somewhere along the way we were taught that tough love works. If we are hard on ourselves, then somehow we will shame ourselves into better performance, more productivity, and less anxiety. In reality, it's really the opposite that works. People who have more self-compassion are found to be healthier and more productive. I once heard the saying that you can't rebuild a city when it is still under attack and bombardment. It's only once the attacks stop and peace prevails that the rebuilding can occur. The same goes with our internal world. When we stop criticizing and attacking ourselves and fighting the life we have, only then can we heal and grow as Christians.

Researchers Ethan Kross at the University of Michigan and Jason Moser at Michigan State University have studied how our brains respond to self-talk. They compared what happens when we address ourselves in the third person rather than the first. This means I would start by saying, "Jenna," as though I were speaking to someone other than myself. In one experiment, subjects were asked to recall negative moments from their lives while the researchers monitored their brain activity. The subjects' distress decreased rapidly (within one second!) when they performed self-talk in the third person compared with the first person.

Self-compassion is a concept of offering compassion or concern for suffering for yourself in the same way you would be sympathetic for the misfortunes of others. Self-compassion focuses on soothing and comforting the self when faced with distressing experiences. How can you offer grace to yourself when you don't react the way you want to? How can you remain calm and balanced when you fail? How can you accept your imperfections in less-than-ideal circumstances?

From this perspective, you can start to see how compassion for yourself can be integrated with a Christian worldview. As Christians, we recognize that we are sinners. We also recognize the reality that we live in a fallen and imperfect world. How will we live and cope with that reality on a day-to-day basis without succumbing to self-hatred or discouragement? Self-compassion can be part of the answer. Colossians 3:12 reminds us that we are **"God's chosen people, holy and dearly loved"** and that we are to **"clothe** [ourselves] **with compassion, kindness, humility, gentleness and patience."** It matters that we take care of ourselves and are kind to ourselves because we are God's children. We take care of ourselves so we can serve God and our neighbor.

CHAPTER 3

WHO AM I? THE ROLE OF IDENTITY IN WELLNESS

"God's own child. I'll gladly say it.
I am baptized into Christ!"[1]

"Today you are you! That is truer than true!
There is no one alive who is you-er than you!
Shout loud, 'I am lucky to be what I am.'"[2]
—Dr. Seuss

Identity is a critical indicator of behavior. How we identify is a strong indicator of what we do. I'm not just talking about gender identity or sexual orientation but all the labels and words we have about ourselves that indicate how we view ourselves. *Oxford Languages* defines *identity* as the "fact of being who or what a person or thing is." Identity is the fact of you being who you are. The word comes from Latin, and it literally means "your repeated beingness." It isn't just about your persona online or your personal branding; it's about who you are at your core. There's a Latin phrase that seems to sum up this concept well: *esse quam videri*, which means "to *be* rather than to *seem*." I once heard the concept that the most powerful force in the human personality is the need to stay consistent with how we define ourselves. Understanding our personal definitions of ourselves is critical to be aware of, because we strive as humans to operate in alignment with how we define ourselves. But how does your repeated beingness develop? What makes you who you are?

You are redeemed by Christ with his blood. God sees you in Christ's image and in many beautiful and unique ways. First Peter 2:9 says, **"But you are a chosen people, a royal priesthood, a holy nation, God's special possession."** What a beautiful reminder that you and I are chosen, royal, holy, and special. Ephesians 2:10 describes us as God's handiwork, and John 1:12 reminds us that we are children of God. Romans 8:17 expands on that and states that if we are children, then we are also heirs. The definition of the word *heir* is especially powerful. It is defined in *Oxford Languages* as "a person legally entitled to the property or rank of another on that person's death" That is a special, unique, honorable position to be in, but it is absolutely priceless to be the heir of God himself!

First Corinthians 12:27 reminds us that we are the body of Christ and each one of us is a part of it. First Corinthians 6:19 describes our bodies as temples of the Holy Spirit. We are so cherished by God. We were made by him in his image. It is comforting and awe-inspiring to be reminded of how revered we are by God himself. It makes any worldly identity pale in comparison to how God sees us and who we are through faith in him. And we must remember to look at our worldly labels in light of what God says about us first.

Our worldly labels and identities typically start to develop early on and evolve based on the feedback we receive from our primary caregivers and those early in our lives. Our identities are critical because they implicate what we think, how we feel, what we are and aren't willing to do, and the habits and behaviors we engage in. What complicates this even further is that they sometimes evolve based on how we think others perceive us.

In 1902 the sociologist Charles Horton Cooley wrote, "I am not what I think I am, and I am not what you think I am. I am what I think you think I am." Our identities are wrapped up in what others think of us or, more accurately, what we *think* others think of us. Cooley called this phenomenon the "looking-glass self." Not only are our self-images tied up in how we think others see us, but most of our efforts at self-improvement can become attempts of trying to meet that imagined ideal.

We form our identities based on what we believe others think of us. It's fascinating. It's powerful. If you are the oldest child and take care of everyone, you are likely to be labeled and perceived as the caregiver, as the responsible one, the one who is dependable and trustworthy. You start to get this feedback from parents and peers, and this is how you perceive others think you are. You might become the one who tells on others who are misbehaving in school. Or you might be the designated sober driver in college. In adulthood you might become the one who hosts every family gathering and sends out color-coded lists of what everyone should bring.

Many times our labels are protective for us, and they make us who we are. We identify as Christians, so we go to church every Sunday, pray before we eat, and read devotions every night. If we identify as atheists, our behavior looks very different. We might identify as "creative" or "Type A" or "a slacker" or a "cheesehead" or "outdoorsy" or an "awesome cook."

Sometimes we carry labels that developed in our childhood or adolescence that might not be true anymore. Sometimes we develop labels that are self-critical or simply cruel to ourselves: "I'm a stupid loser" or, "I'm a dumb farm boy" or, "I'm a crazy psycho who doesn't make any sense."

Lots of labels from the past may hold us back. If you received feedback from a certain teacher that you weren't smart, you likely self-selected yourself out of going to medical school. If you got feedback from others that you weren't organized or weren't careful or were disruptive, this shaped how you saw yourself.

It is important to think about what labels simply aren't true. Many are fictional and given to us by society. Take some time to ponder this. What if you are good at art but you never believed you were? What if you are athletic even though you weren't a jock in high school? What if you can influence people even though you think of yourself as introverted and quiet? It's important for us to become conscious of the identities we align with.

REFLECTION BREAK

Take a minute and think of ten labels that are in alignment with how you define yourself. List them:

How do these labels impact your behavior?

How are they strengths?

How do they hold you back?

Let's focus on how our identities might impede our growth and hold us back. If you identify as a die-hard Vikings football fan and the Vikings lose, how do you feel? How do you treat your family differently? They say that the testosterone of sports fans drops when their teams lose, and this in turn can make men irritable and aggressive. Overidentifying with a sports team can be a barrier to relationships or becoming our best selves. If we become too strongly attached to our labels, it can leave us feeling fragile and exposed. If we were to lose them for any reason, we'd lose our sense of who we are.

Take my label as a professor. What if I got sick and was unable to work any longer? What if I got fired from my job? Who would I be then? How would I feel about myself if my whole identity was wrapped up in the idea of being a professor and I could no longer be one? This often happens when people retire. Their happiness and health start to go downhill because they've lost their sense of self and no longer identify with the role they had in their careers.

I once did an identity exercise in a training I hosted for clinical mental health providers. When I asked about how our identities can be protective or detrimental to us professionally, a participant in my training, who was about a 50-year-old white male, brought up a great example. He said that he identifies as a farm boy, and this has always meant that he is dependable, hardworking, and determined. He is a fabulous employee. He is always on time, always gets his paperwork completed, and is at the office no matter the weather. He aligns strongly with this farm boy mentality, and it has served him well professionally. At the same time, this identification with being a farm boy and having those values also has setbacks. He comes off as rigid and judgmental to younger employees. He doesn't have understanding or empathy if his coworkers take a sick day or get to work late. He doesn't understand other personality types that may be more flexible and easier going. It was a powerful moment for him in the training to gain this awareness about himself and how his identity as a farm boy could be a great strength for him but could also hold him back in other ways.

Some of these labels and perceptions of ourselves might be old, or there may be barriers to identities we would like to develop. After doing a lot of thinking and reflection, I realized that I have never identified as a "healthy person." Healthy people equaled the people who made me feel guilty when I'm eating cheese dip and drinking margaritas at a Mexican restaurant. When I thought of healthy people, I thought of people who were demonized in the media as the moms who only bring organic and non-GMO food to bake sales, only eat kale, and make everyone else feel like a slob. *Healthy* to me meant disconnection, feeling left out, and not having fun, all things that are counterintuitive to my nature.

In reality, I frequently do the Whole30 food plan to reset my body and brain. I fast every day and drink bulletproof coffee for breakfast, and I work out and sit in a sauna between five and seven times per week. I was living as a healthy person but still had a barrier to identifying as one. I know this sounds weird, but it was profound for me to uncover. Once I embraced the identity of being healthy, maintaining good habits was easier. It wasn't about what I did; it was about *who I was.*

What's interesting about our identities, as James Clear points out in his book *Atomic Habits*, is that we tend to engage in behaviors that most support the identities we are most proud of. My sister is a runner. In fact, in November 2022 she ran four marathons in four days in four different states! Yes, you read that correctly. Four marathons in four days. She is a runner. That is part of who she is, and it is a part that she is and should be very proud of. Because she is a runner, she runs nearly every day. When I talked to her after she got back from her trip, she was on her way to the gym to go running.

I, on the other hand, do not identify as a runner but strongly identify as a reader. I read to my children every day. I read by myself every day as well, for at least 20 minutes before bed. I'm proud of this identity. I consider reading to be a powerful venue to professional growth, which is one of my core values. Reading a variety of books greatly informs my professional work and gives me a lot of interesting things to talk to my husband and friends and colleagues about. Reading with my children is a beautiful bonding time, and we learn new words and fall in love with the characters of our series together.

Personal and professional growth can occur when you can develop identities you are proud of. Our true identities stem from a foundation as redeemed children of God. Knowing that, when you ask yourself, "Who do I want to become?" you can gain further clarity for the ways in which you would like to grow. That is when your brain starts to create a picture of your ideal self and you can work toward growing into that person. This is a technique called the "best self." This comes from Yale Center for Emotional Intelligence Director Marc Brackett in his book *Permission to Feel*. Simply put, the best self is an ideal that we can think about and live up to. It's a picture of the person we are working toward becoming, and it's a continual process to close the gap between where we are and where we would like to be. It's an idealized version of ourselves. When I think about my best self, I think about being very calm and present with whomever and whatever I am doing at the time. I think about making people feel like they matter. My best self soaks in moments with my kids and continually offers gratitude and appreciation for my husband. I am constantly working on becoming more calm, present, and appreciative, and that is okay. I have a clear intention of who I want to become.

REFLECTION BREAK

1. Describe your best self. You might think of adjectives or even an image that helps your best self appear to you. You might also think about your reputation: How do you want to be seen, talked about, or experienced? How do you behave when someone you respect is watching?

2. Your personal identity comes from your values. Your personal values are another important indicator of your behavior. Values are the beliefs that are most important to you, and they help you clarify what matters to you. They help your behavior stay in alignment with what you cherish the most. Think about this for a bit and jot down some things you value and cherish. Turn the page for more guidance.

3. So what do you truly value in life? Below I've listed some possible values to help you. This is not an exhaustive list, so use it as a guide only and feel free to add your own. Choose two values:

Accountability	Curiosity	Independence
Achievement	Dignity	Initiative
Activism	Diversity	Integrity
Adaptability	Environment	Intuition
Adventure	Equality	Joy
Altruism	Excellence	Justice
Ambition	Faith	Kindness
Authenticity	Family	Knowledge
Balance	Forgiveness	Leadership
Beauty	Freedom	Learning
Being the best	Friendship	Legacy
Belonging	Fun	Leisure
Career	Generosity	Love
Caring	Giving back	Loyalty
Collaboration	Gratitude	Making a difference
Commitment	Growth	Nature
Community	Harmony	Openness
Compassion	Health	Optimism
Connection	Home	Order
Contentment	Honesty	Parenting
Contribution	Hope	Patience
Courage	Humility	Patriotism
Creativity	Humor	Peace

Perseverance	Self-respect	Trust
Personal fulfillment	Serenity	Truth
Power	Service	Understanding
Pride	Simplicity	Vision
Reliability	Spirituality	Vulnerability
Resourcefulness	Stewardship	Wealth
Respect	Success	Well-being
Responsibility	Teamwork	Wholeheartedness
Risk taking	Time	Wisdom
Security	Tradition	
Self-discipline	Travel	

Write your own:

VALUE #1:

Think of a time when you were operating in alignment with this value? What was happening for you? How did it feel? How were you behaving?

Think of a time when you were operating out of alignment with this value? What was happening for you? How did it feel? How were you behaving?

What do you need to do to create more alignment with this value?

VALUE #2:

Think of a time when you were operating in alignment with this value? What was happening for you? How did it feel? How were you behaving?

Think of a time when you were operating out of alignment with this value? What was happening for you? How did it feel? How were you behaving?

What do you need to do to create more alignment with this value?

This process of consciously defining your identity is critically important because it helps you develop alignment. Alignment is when your inner values and external actions match up with one another. But how do you know if you are operating in alignment if you have never taken the time to define what your values are in the first place? The values exercise is incredibly powerful and designed to help you assess your internal values. Once you have done this, you will be able to see if your day-to-day behaviors match up with them. Do you say that you value undistracted time with your family yet your real-world evidence shows that you hardly have any at all? Do you say that you value your health, yet on reflection you never have time for self-care? Do you say that you value your close friends, when in reality you have not found time to catch up and connect with them in the past six months?

It is important to remember that the values exercise is unique to you. It is critical to gain awareness and ensure your actions are matching up with your values. Over time, these exercises can help you tweak your daily behaviors so that you can become more aligned, which can have transformative effects on your faith, health, and happiness. Clarifying who you are and who you want to become is a helpful exercise along with remembering that you are a child of God first and foremost.

CHAPTER 4
THE MIND

"Do not conform to the pattern of this world,
but be transformed by the renewing of your mind.
Then you will be able to test and approve what God's
will is—his good, pleasing and perfect will."
Romans 12:2

"All problems are illusions of the mind."[1]
—Eckhart Tolle

The "mind" is an odd concept. We talk about it a lot, but no one can really define it clearly. We say, "He's out of his mind." Or, "I'm losing my mind." We talk about mindset or mindfulness, but what are we talking about? What is the mind? What is the brain? What is mental health? And how are we to think about all these things as Christians?

The analysis of the mind was first brought into modern psychology by Freud and has been done widely ever since. From identifying problematic thought patterns, the idea of the "subconscious," the analysis of emotions and the workings of memory to studying the symptoms of mental illness, we are heavily focused on the brain and the mind. The mind is considered to be associated with the brain, and the terms *brain* and *mind* are often used interchangeably.

The brain is composed of nerve cells and is a physical thing that can be touched, whereas the mind is "mental" and cannot be touched. The brain gives rise to the mind. The mind uses the brain, and the brain responds to the mind. The mind generates energy through thinking, feeling, and choosing and has been described as our "aliveness," without which the physical brain and body would be useless. It reminds me of someone who might be in a coma and whose physical body and brain are functioning, but they are not themselves; they are not their alive selves. That person's mind and brain have been damaged.

The mind in action creates energy in the brain, and it can be measured by neuroscientists. Your mind is your thoughts, feelings, and the meanings you make of your situation. Your mind is the conclusions you draw.

The Center for Disease Control (CDC) says mental health "includes our emotional, psychological, and social well-being. It affects how we think, feel, and act. It also helps determine how we handle stress, relate to others, and make healthy choices." It states, "Mental health is important at every stage of life, from childhood and adolescence through adulthood."[2] We know that people struggle with their mental health, but it can be hard to understand tangibly what that means.

Mental health diagnoses are clusters of symptoms that have to occur for several months and cause you significant impairment in your functioning. There are a variety of types of mental health challenges, with the most common diagnoses being depression and anxiety. The Mayo Clinic defines depression as "a mood disorder that causes a persistent feeling of sadness and loss of interest. . . . It affects how you feel, think and behave."[3] Other symptoms include tiredness and lack of energy, slowed thinking, irritability, loss of pleasure, and feelings of worthlessness or guilt to name a few. A new study from the *American Journal of Preventive Medicine* found that nearly 10% of Americans suffer from symptoms of depression, with the mood disorder increasing fastest among teens and young adults.[4]

Anxiety disorders are characterized by having a persistent feeling of anxiety or dread; difficulty controlling feelings of worry; feeling restless; having difficulty concentrating; being wound up, irritable, or on edge; and having these feelings interfere with a person's daily life. Anxiety disorders are the most common mental illness in the U.S., affecting 40 million adults (19.1% of the population).

There are many factors that contribute to these symptoms, and a multifaceted approach to treatment is wise. If you are experiencing the symptoms mentioned above and have been for an extended period of time, I would recommend meeting with a mental health professional to receive support. The foundations of health—including restorative sleep, daily movement, eating whole foods, being in nature, and social connection—are a great place to start improving if you are experiencing these symptoms.

It is also imperative to know that there are many physical health symptoms that may manifest as mental health symptoms. Our hormones, vitamins and minerals, environment, and exposure to toxins can create symptoms that mirror mental health disorders such as anxiety and depression. Getting as much information as you can about your body can help you discover the origins of your symptoms. Having low levels or issues absorbing minerals, magnesium, vitamins D and K, and B vitamins can cause symptoms. Leaky gut, thyroid problems, high levels of mercury, exposure to toxic mold, or issues with the functioning of your testosterone or estrogen/progesterone can greatly impact your energy and mind.

I had a student who was struggling with symptoms of sadness, low energy, fatigue, and muscle weakness, and it turned out to be a vitamin D deficiency, not depression. There is no amount of therapy that could have helped her with the underlying cause of her issues. It is critical to get your bodily health in order as a foundation for building your mental and emotional health.

Understanding the common disorders that affect

our minds and the trends in mental health is important. There are also many practices you can engage in to protect your mind and optimize your mental health through your thought patterns.

GAIN AWARENESS OF YOUR THOUGHT PATTERNS

One idea that changed my life regarding mental health is this: we have a choice as to what we focus on, and the first step in that process is gaining awareness into our own thought processes.

During the COVID lockdown, I had a habit of taking long walks in the evening after my kids were in bed. While I walked, I thought and listened to podcasts. I had listened to a podcast that focused on having insight into the thoughts in our heads and how awareness of them is critical. I had heard that idea before as a mental health therapist, but I never intentionally tried it myself. I had never really been still with my thoughts and simply watched them. The podcast talked about how a critical part of this practice is not judging yourself for what you find but just noticing. I began practicing being quiet in my own mind. That is how I began to notice what I was thinking. This was a shocking discovery. In a way, it was like a mirror had been held up to my sinful self. I noticed how I could be judgmental or have unrealistic expectations for people. I saw my own greed and my own selfishness and my own negative thinking. It was a powerful reminder that even though sometimes I feel like I'm a good person, I'm sinful and I need my Savior.

Meditation is a popular topic in modern psychology and mainstream neuroscience. It is estimated that we think between 60,000 and 90,000 thoughts per day, with most of them being the same thoughts we had the previous day and most of them being negative or pessimistic. I never knew that we could control our thoughts—not like mind control or something, but we have the power to have an awareness of the thoughts we think. All healthy humans have an inner stream of thoughts and feelings that include criticism, doubt, and fear. That's just our minds doing the job they were designed to do: try to anticipate and solve problems and avoid dangers and pitfalls. Thankfully, we have the power to challenge our thoughts. Most of our thoughts are automatic. We don't consciously develop a conclusion; the thought just pops into our minds.

The power we have is to become aware of our thinking patterns and the conclusions and meanings we give to our experiences. For instance, if someone cuts you off in traffic, your automatic thought may be, "What a jerk! He has no regard for anyone around him." If you drive past this person and see he is elderly, you may think to yourself, "That old geezer shouldn't be driving. His kids should take away his license!" This reminds me of a story of my friend who was nine months pregnant with twins and sobbing as she was driving slowly down the road. The person in the car next to her honked at her and then flipped her off as he or she drove past. It ended up being someone my friend knew! The person who honked and flipped my friend off was mortified and apologized profusely, but it goes to show that we never know what anyone is experiencing. Our brains automatically tell us that whoever offends us on the road is inherently a bad person. Our bodies respond with a cascade of chemicals that put us into fight-or-flight mode. The stress hormone cortisol is released in our brains, and our breath becomes short and shallow. Our heart rates increase, and our palms may become sweaty. This is when we react out of anger, and thus the phenomena "road rage" is born.

It is crazy how thoughts impact our bodies and how we can change our biology just by a few simple tweaks. We may automatically react with road rage, but we can catch ourselves. I was once driving all my kids to school and drove past a bus that was trying to turn. The driver yelled out his window, "You stupid idiot!" My kids and I were both shocked, and we actually got it on tape with our dashcam. Although my instinct was to say, "What a weirdo. That guy shouldn't be driving kids around with such an overactivated stress response," it turned out to be an awesome opportunity not only to regulate my reaction in the moment but talk to my kids about it. We talked about the fact that the bus driver was likely struggling and dealing with a lot of stress. We talked about how it must have felt for the kids on the bus to hear language like that, and we actually said a prayer before I dropped them off at school. It would have been easy to feel like a victim and think negative thoughts about him all day, but instead it was an opportunity to cultivate forgiveness, empathy, tools to regulate our emotions, and a stronger prayer life. Not a bad tradeoff for being called an idiot.

GUARD YOUR MIND

When I give self-care trainings, one piece of advice that I offer is to guard your mind. I originally heard this from Tony Robbins, who heard it from his mentor, Jim Rohn. I thought about what my mom said to us kids constantly in our childhood: "Garbage in, garbage out." She said this a lot of times when I was caught watching trashy talk shows after school. My parents were intentional (strict) about the media we could consume as kids, and thankfully smartphones weren't around in my prime neurodevelopmental years. I couldn't watch PG-13 movies until I was 13, which was unfortunate for me because *Titanic* came out in theaters when I was 12. I remember renting the movie *Spice World* with my friends for a sleepover. My mom said that she didn't want us to watch it because it wasn't quality media and the image being promoted wasn't a Christ-like image she was comfortable with us having. While growing up, at times I felt major FOMO (fear of missing out) due to missing some movies and shows that my friends were watching. Now I couldn't be more thankful to my parents for not exposing me to media that impacted my thoughts, feelings, and focus. Garbage in, garbage out is real, especially in our social media, digital world. It is impacting our brains and our minds at an alarming rate. Our minds are not being guarded. They are exposed to every shooting, every tragedy, every murder, every war, every injustice, and everyone's opinion about all of it. We have young people who are live streaming themselves as they end their own lives. The suicide rate is the highest it has been in the past century, and mental health is declining.

Our brains and minds are also impacted by trauma. Trauma has been described as any pattern of stress that activates our nervous systems and leads to an overactivity or an over-reactivity in our brains. Historically, we have thought about trauma in war veterans or those who have been in an accident or a natural disaster. For a while in the mental health world, trauma was overused and every training focused on trauma. In the post-COVID world, we are seeing that many people changed in their stress response.

When our stress response is activated, it releases a neurochemical called cortisol. This is a functional response that helps keep us safe when we perceive a threat. It alerts our bodies to fight or flee from danger. What happens in modern day is that our brains don't do a great job of making a distinction between "threat" and "danger," and they give us a signal that we are in danger when the input we are receiving isn't an actual threat.

In thinking about the recent pandemic and how that caused extreme discord in our families and around the country, a lasting impact among many is the stress of feeling unsafe and living in disharmony. If someone you loved disagreed with you about COVID laws, rules, restrictions, or regulations, I'm guessing you may have experienced some conflict. No matter what you believe about it, it is stressful to experience conflict, and your stress response is activated when you do. Now if that loved one calls you on the phone, just seeing that person's name might send a cortisol response to your brain.

Our stress response system is constantly activated by social media and stressful news headlines as well. Our brains are designed to keep us safe, not make us happy, so when we see ambiguous headlines that insinuate danger or threat to us, it is biologically instinctual that we keep reading. The news capitalizes on this neurobiology and brings up the worst things possible to keep us reading. So guard your mind. The garbage our minds are consuming is not sustainable for mental health and wellness. I'm not saying that you can't look at the news or talk about hard things, but be intentional about how you communicate them and what you focus on.

RESIST A VICTIM MENTALITY AND NEGATIVE THOUGHT PATTERNS

Complaining also releases cortisol. It's not healthy for you. It may feel cathartic to vent or complain in the moment, but it is inherently stressful not only for you but also for the recipient of your complaining. Complaining is especially stressful for men, and they have found that exposure to complaining actually lowers their testosterone. You think that men with high testosterone are aggressive and lash out like the hulk, but it is actually the opposite. Men with low levels of testosterone tend to be more irritable and aggressive.[5] Who would have thought that estrogen is the aggressive hormone!

In hard times, many people bond by complaining. There is so much content there; you're never at a loss for conversation if you talk about all the stupid people out there and all the ways the government or your boss or your kids or the people of Walmart have wronged you. There was actually a study done that looked at the impact of complaining. Stanford psychologists took 104 subjects and assigned them to one of two groups—one group was told to write a short essay about a time they were bored and the other to write about a time when life seemed unfair or when they felt wronged or slighted by someone. Afterward, the participants were asked if they wanted to help the researchers with an easy task. Those who had written about a time they had been wronged or slighted were 26% less likely to help the researchers. They were also more likely to steal the researchers pens and leave trash behind!

The main finding of the study was that complaining gives us what is called the victim's mentality, where we see ourselves as victims in a situation. They said that this mentality can leave us feeling selfish and entitled. We are in survival mode, and that makes us inherently selfish. We don't help others when we are in survival mode. We don't see the perspective of others or have empathy. We focus on us and our needs and wants.

During COVID, I made a point to still have an option to have my college courses in person, as well as online. I remember being in the office in a building that had literally no one else in it and thinking to myself, "Why am I the only one who cares?" That's not a good question. If you ask yourself a question, your brain will give you an answer—remember, it hates ambiguity! So when I ask myself, "Why am I the only one who cares?" my brain will give me a critical and selfish answer: "I don't know; you're on your own." Or, "No one works as hard as you." I also remember being asked to join certain committees around that time and thinking, "Nope, I'm not doing any more work. I work harder than anyone here anyway." Victim mentality. Remember, that makes us entitled and selfish, not exactly the best version of ourselves.

Comparing ourselves to others or judging ourselves can also create a victim mindset. When we compare our experience with anyone else and think that we don't have a right to feel a certain way because we "don't have it so bad," this kind of comparison can lead us to minimize or diminish our own suffering. Surviving and thriving through hardship requires absolute acceptance of what was and what is. If we discount our pain or punish ourselves for feeling lost, isolated, or scared about the challenges in our lives, however insignificant these challenges may seem to someone else, then we are still choosing to be victims. We're not seeing our choice. We're judging ourselves. As Holocaust survivor Edith Eger says, "I don't want you to hear my story and say, 'My own suffering is less significant.' I want you to hear my story and say, 'If she can do it, then so can I!'"[6]

It's also important to have some insight into thought patterns that are creating distress. Once again, you have the power to notice them and change them! For example, what are some thoughts you may have if . . .

- you look at your bank account and it shows less money than you were expecting.

- you were gone all day and no one emptied the dishwasher despite the fact that your whole family is home and capable of doing so. The dirty dishes are piling up.

- a coworker rolls her eyes when you speak up in a meeting.

- your child says, "You're acting like our boss. And you're a really bad boss." (True story for me.)

A negative thought pattern is easy to develop in any of these situations. Money is specifically a challenging topic because the lack of money can activate a strong fight-or-flight response in people because they truly perceive their survival is at stake when there is a scarcity. The lack of money triggers fear in some people, and they often react irrationally when discussing it. This is a challenging topic especially for couples. If you look at your account and see less than you expect, you may have a whole neurological pathway of anger, frustration, resentment toward your spouse, fear, and a whole slew of negative thoughts. Sometimes our thoughts are simply irrational. You might think, "I should have married someone rich." Or, "I wish we had more discipline." Or, "You spend so much because you were an entitled rich kid growing up." This lack of finances may trigger your thoughts to become so heated that you attack your spouse as a person and criticize core aspects of their identity out of your perception and fear.

I remember a couple coming to me for therapy because the wife had racked up a $3,000 credit card bill at Kohl's. Although the couple had enough in their savings to cover the expense, the husband was so upset that they needed professional help to manage this situation.

COMMUNICATE SAFETY TO YOUR BODY

When you are triggered, it's imperative that you have some insight into the fear you are feeling and the conclusions you are making. The most effective way to deal with fear is by communicating safety to your body, which can be quickly or automatically triggered into fight or flight. You see a low account balance, and your heart rate is automatically increased. One of the best tools that modern psychology has given us is a pause. Sometimes we expect complex and innovative solutions to the problems we face, but when your thoughts become frustrated, resentful, or angry, the best thing you can do is close your mouth before addressing the situation. Literally, just pause and do whatever you can to regulate your body so your mind will follow suit. I will list several ways to do this at the end of this chapter.

I once worked at a clinic with a group of clients with addiction, and we talked about how reacting to situations can have detrimental outcomes. My clients discussed that when they reacted without pausing, it led to some of the worst imagined outcomes. They relapsed or overdosed on drugs and alcohol. They assaulted their friends and loved ones. One client talked about impulsively attempting suicide. Some discussed how their lack of a pause led them to be sentenced to jail and even to prison. Years of recovery went down the drain when they reacted by using drugs or alcohol. Not to mention the words that were said to their children and loved ones. It makes me think of how we should never make a permanent decision based on our temporary feelings. Taking a pause and regulating your body before you act can change your life.

It's also very effective to solve problems in our minds by regulating our bodies and asking for help from God. It doesn't always work to generate problems of the mind with solutions from the mind. When you are generating solutions from the mind, I think the first step is to become aware of what you are thinking. Then, a model of analyzing your thoughts (originally developed by Byron Katie but adapted by Daniel Amen) is to ask yourself if this thought is true. It might feel weird to do this because you probably think your thoughts are true. But ask yourself if this thought is absolutely true. Then consider how you would feel if you didn't have this thought at all. Dr. Daniel Amen, a pioneer in brain health research, recommends his patients take their top one hundred negative thoughts and analyze them with this model. It's pretty intense, but you can see how it can transform your brain, body, and mind.[7]

EXERCISE

Step one
Think a thought that makes you feel bad. Write it down.

Step two
Considering this painful thought, ask the following four questions.

    1. Is it true?
    2. Is it absolutely true?

3. How do I react? What happens when I believe that thought?

4. Who or what would I be without the thought?

CONSIDER YOUR FOCUS

Modern psychology and neurobiology now discuss in depth how our brains can rewire themselves based on our experiences. Historically, we thought that we were born with the brains we had, but we know that our brains change based on our feelings, our environment, our thinking, our interactions, and even our eating. That is why trauma can impact the brain. We also know that focus is very important, because when it comes to your brain, they say that where focus goes, energy flows. And what you focus on, strengthens. If your focus is "I'm a bad mom; I'm a bad mom; I'm a bad mom," that belief is going to strengthen, even if it is completely false. Your brain is going to look for ways to be compatible with that belief; thus, it will be extra aware of the data that confirms that you are a bad mom. Same goes for thoughts of your spouse, your parents, your kids, your neighbors, the people who believe the opposite of what you do politically, and your thoughts about your crazy relatives who rant on Facebook. It is critically imperative for your mental health that you are aware of what you focus on and where you direct your mental energy.

God also discusses the importance of your mind and your focus. In Philippians 4:8 he says, **"Finally, brothers** and sisters, whatever is true, whatever is noble, whatever is right, whatever is pure, whatever is lovely, whatever is admirable—if anything is excellent or praiseworthy—think about such things." Wow! Think of how different the world would be if we all focused our minds on topics that had these qualities. The devil, the world, and our own sinful selves encourage us to think about whatever is new, whatever is crazy, whatever is frightening, whatever is frustrating, whatever is popular, whatever is infuriating, whatever leads to despair.

Direct your mind to the content and the areas described in Philippians 4:8. How can you focus on whatever is true, noble, right, pure, lovely, admirable, excellent, and praiseworthy? How can you encourage your families to focus on things that have these qualities? How can you do this from a place of joy and excitement, instead of out of duty or guilt? God has a framework for the types of things he wants us to think about. He knows neurobiology better than anyone. He designed and created our brains. He knows the importance of what we think about and how that influences our feelings, our bodies, our brains, and our behaviors. When you look at your bank account and see a low number, how can you think about what is true? God's got you. God will take care of you. God is using this as an opportunity to shape you.

What we know about the brain is that it can change based on what we think. Our bodies can change based on what we think. We can think ourselves into a panic attack. That doesn't mean our panic isn't real; it means our minds are powerful.

Here are examples of thoughts from Philippians 4:8 that can help you focus:

What is true: God is good. He is in control of my life. He will protect me. I can handle hard things through him who gives me strength.

Whatever is noble. I will do the right thing even when no one is looking. I am a strong Christian, and I will show my faith out of love for God. I work hard and protect those around me.

What is right. I will forgive this person because God forgives me. That was a hard situation, but I'm choosing to show this person love because God loves me. Even though I am overwhelmed, I'm going to react in a peaceful and loving manner.

What is pure. God loves me. Love is the greatest fruit of the Spirit. I love my husband/wife, and I will honor them with what I think and do. I am cleansed through the washing of regeneration and renewal of the Holy Spirit. Love is all you need (wait, that's the Beatles).

Whatever is lovely. I will love and serve God and my neighbor. I will show others love and let the love of Christ radiate from me.

Whatever is admirable. God gives me courage to do the right thing. I work hard and have discipline to honor God.

If anything is excellent and praiseworthy. God grants me opportunities to have a beautiful marriage and create a safe and joyful home with my family. God gives me strengths and abilities to make an impact in the world he has created. I am able to work hard and praise him with my God-given talents and serve him joyfully in this world. He gives me the peace that surpasses all understanding—to him be the glory!

Our minds are powerful, and there are many ways that we can protect our minds from the world. Guarding our minds; communicating safety to our bodies when we feel upset; being intentional about our thinking; and keeping our focus on whatever is true, noble, right, pure, lovely, excellent, and praiseworthy is a great place to start. Our thoughts, our feelings, and our situations will begin to transform when we shift our focus from the fear of the world to the love of God.

CHAPTER 5
EMOTIONS

"Do not be anxious about anything, but in every situation, by prayer and petition, with thanksgiving, present your requests to God. And the peace of God, which transcends all understanding, will guard your hearts and your minds in Christ Jesus."
Philippians 4:6,7

"Anything that's human is mentionable, and anything that is mentionable can be manageable. When we can talk about our feelings, they become less overwhelming, less upsetting, less scary. The people we trust with that important talk can help us know that we are not alone."[1]
—Fred Rogers

Emotions are a beautiful part of who we are as humans. They help us feel things deeply, have love and empathy for others, give us the ability to comfort and soothe, and help us connect to our families and communities. Author Marc Brackett states, "Our multiple senses bring us news from our bodies, our minds, and the outside world, and then our brains process and analyze it and formulate our experience. We call that a feeling."[2]

Emotions are a critical part of mental wellness, and many people struggle with negative and overwhelming emotions. Oftentimes people will do anything to escape the feelings they have. It is important to understand that emotions are an important source of information about what is going on inside of us. While we can't spend all day focused on how we feel, we also can't go through life ignoring what we feel or minimizing our experiences.

All of us have ideas about "good" emotions and "bad" emotions, and we live in a culture that overwhelmingly wants not to feel the bad feelings. The immediate gratification culture teaches us that if we feel any sort of discomfort, we can easily and quickly "fix" it. When we do feel the bad emotions like sad, lonely, frustrated, disheartened, or even despair, we feel like there is something inherently wrong with us. We go on social media and look at the awesome lives of everyone else, and we begin to believe we are the only ones who feel this way. Sometimes, even as Christians, when we struggle with overwhelming emotions, we are told to just pray and to trust in God and to know our feelings aren't real. We may feel like we aren't good enough Christians or our prayers aren't working. It is difficult for us to admit that we are not okay. C. S. Lewis once observed, "The frequent attempt to conceal mental pain increases the burden: It is easier to say 'My tooth is aching' than to say 'My heart is broken.'"[3]

Our society has a long history of disregarding feelings. We think of intelligence and emotion as coming from two completely different parts of our bodies: our heads and our hearts. Which of the two have we been taught to trust the most? Emotions can't be measured with standardized tests the way that intelligence can be measured. IQ relies on cognitive processes such as remembering facts and digits, while emotional intelligence relies on social-emotional processes that focus on evaluating, predicting, and coping with feelings and behaviors—our own and other people's. A formal theory of emotional intelligence was developed in 1990 and was defined as the "ability to monitor one's own and others' feelings and emotions, to discriminate among them and to use this information to guide one's thinking and actions."[4]

Emotions play a critical role in attention, memory, and learning. If you are bored to tears or daydreaming about the weekend, you're less likely to absorb the information you are learning. If you are fearful, the source of the fear occupies all your thoughts. Even fear of intangible harm like embarrassment, shame, or looking foolish works in a similar way. The emotion may seem silly or vain, but it doesn't matter. Emotions don't respond to cold logic.

In education, emotions impact the students' abilities to learn. Students are tired, bored, and stressed. Their teachers are frustrated, pressured, and overwhelmed.

The research tells us that emotions determine whether academic content will be processed deeply and remembered. Linking emotion to learning ensures that the instruction is relevant. Emotion is what helps people discover their purpose and passion, and it's what drives their persistence.

Emotion is also critical for decision-making. We believe that our ability to reason and think rationally is our highest mental power, above our unruly emotional side. In reality, emotions exert a huge influence over how our minds function and largely determine our actions. If we are feeling something positive—confidence, optimism, contentment—we'll come to one conclusion about what we ought to do. If we are feeling negative feelings like anxiety, anger, or sadness, our decision might be completely different, even with the same set of facts. Anxiety narrows our attention and improves our focus on details. It makes us anticipate what could go wrong. This may not sound like a desirable state, but it's a good frame of mind if you are working on your taxes or filling out a job application. Negative emotions make us weigh facts carefully and err on the side of caution to protect ourselves.

The role of emotion in decision-making has been studied scientifically in a number of studies. In one study out of Yale, the researchers took two groups of teachers and had one group recall a negative classroom experience and the other group recall a positive classroom experience. They were all then asked to grade the same middle school essay. The positive-mood group marked the essay a full grade higher than the negative-mood group, although the majority of teachers report that they don't believe their mood affects how they evaluate papers.

In another study, participants were made to feel sad, and they reported perceiving a mountain to be steeper than it actually was. Another study on medical school admissions found that applicants were more likely to be admitted on sunny days than when it rained. Emotions are powerful, and they influence us in many ways, even in ways that we aren't conscious of. Instead of trying to suppress your feelings, criticizing yourself for feeling the way you do, or numbing your feelings through any possible means, noticing your feelings with curiosity is a great place to start. When you begin to notice them without judgment or shame, they start to feel less heavy.

Another foundational concept about emotions that is a cornerstone for emotional wellness is the idea that all feelings matter, and the "bad" feelings serve incredibly important functions in our lives. Guilt lets us know that we are doing something wrong and that we need to change our behavior. Anxiety gives us information that we are facing a threat and need to pay attention and be on edge. Grief shows us that we have lost something that we cared about and feel sadness as a result. In the Marvel show *WandaVision*, a character beautifully said, "What is grief, but love persisting?"

It is critically important to notice and honor your

feelings and never criticize yourself for how you feel. Yes, your feelings might be irrational. Yes, they might not make sense. The best thing you can do is approach them with curiosity and self-compassion. Then it is critical that you label your feelings accurately and with nuance. Dr. Susan David, Harvard psychologist and author of *Emotional Agility*, talks about how often we use the umbrella word of *stress*. Your spouse asks how you are, and you say, "I'm so stressed!" Dr. David says that we often use the word *stress* to describe a range of emotional states including anxious, overwhelmed, pressured, disappointed, or depleted. We label all these feelings as "stress." The experience of feeling depleted is different than the experience of feeling overwhelmed. The experience of feeling disappointed is different than feeling pressured. It's important that you develop an emotional vocabulary so your brain knows how to cope. If you can label your emotions with nuance, it also helps you receive support. If you can talk about your disappointment, your significant other or family member may know how to encourage you in a more helpful way than if you call all your feelings "stress."[5]

A growing body of research shows that emotional rigidity—getting hooked by thoughts, feelings, and behaviors that don't serve us—is associated with a range of psychological ills, including depression and anxiety. Meanwhile, emotional agility—being flexible with your thoughts and feelings so you can respond optimally to everyday situations—is key to well-being and success.[6]

Emotional agility supports the approach described by Viktor Frankl, a psychiatrist who survived a Nazi death camp and went on to write *Man's Search for Meaning* about leading a more meaningful life, a life in which our human potential can be fulfilled. He wrote, "Between stimulus and response there is a space. In that space is our power to choose our response. In our response lies our growth and freedom."[7] Although we as Christians know that our true freedom is found in Christ alone, it is important to pause before we react and "open up" the space between how we feel and what we do about those feelings. James 1:19 says, **"My dear brothers and sisters, take note of this: Everyone should be quick to listen, slow to speak and slow to become angry."**

God knows that pausing before we speak in a tense situation can help and also reminds us of the value of listening first.

Sometimes when we try to talk about how we are feeling, the people we talk to minimize or scoff at us, try to fix it, or make the conversation about themselves. No wonder so many people self-medicate their feelings away by any means possible including drugs, alcohol, pornography, overeating, overspending, or in more benign ways like binge-watching TV shows or going on their phones!

When I started to learn more about the science behind feelings, my life changed. The way I thought about and communicated my feelings changed, and I am able to better cope and better receive support than ever before.

A wonderful tool to help label emotions was developed by Marc Brackett and is called the mood meter. Just Google "mood meter," and you'll get all kinds of images for it. I have shared this with clients and students and still frequently use it in presentations about wellness and self-care. The mood meter has a square with four quadrants. Feelings are put into categories with the axes of "pleasantness" and "energy." I think it's important for the goal not to be in high pleasantness/high energy states all the time. That is not realistic, and if someone was always in a high energy/high pleasantness mood, that would get really annoying. You wouldn't want to do your taxes or fill out a job application if you were in that type of mood because you would likely be in a free and easy state and not careful to double-check your work. It often takes high energy/low pleasantness states for change to be made or even for advocacy to occur. We don't analyze or rethink our situations if we are always feeling good. I really like the axes of energy and pleasantness. Now when my husband asks how I am, I will say, "I'm feeling pretty good. I'm low energy but moderate pleasantness." That is good data for him in order to have a pulse as to how I'm doing.

I know a lot of people who feel pressure to perform their jobs in a high energy/high pleasantness state or always try to be in that state when they parent, even if they don't truly feel that way. This need to emotionally "fake it" can often lead to poor health and poor mental health.

Emotions aren't something that need to be "fixed." Maybe you've had a situation where you talked about a problem to someone and that person immediately jumped in and tried to give you a solution. I challenge you: when someone tells you an issue they are struggling with or tells you something hard, just pause for a moment and think about how that must be for them. This is called empathy, which is defined by *Oxford Languages* as "the ability to understand and share the feelings of another."

This can be extremely difficult to do, especially when you have your own feelings to understand, the feelings of the other person are uncomfortable for them to share, and you may feel like you just don't have the time or energy to deal with it all. Most people feel uncomfortable in the face of the suffering of others.

Fred Rogers once pointed out, "People have said, 'Don't cry' to other people for years and years, and all it has ever meant is, 'I'm too uncomfortable when you show your feelings: don't cry.' I'd rather have them say, 'Go ahead and cry. I'm here to be with you.'"[8] Think about how you feel when you see someone who is homeless holding up a sign for money. You might feel uncomfortable. You might feel sad, disgusted, suspicious, or annoyed. It takes courage and emotional discipline to have empathy, and it is one of the greatest gifts you can give to another human. After you have paused and thought about what this person who has shared their challenge is dealing with, think of a word that captures what they just told you. Is it *frustrating*? Is it *overwhelming*? Is it *demoralizing*? All you have to say in response is, "That sounds really overwhelming." You can maybe follow it up with a question about how they are doing with it all or how you can support them. You don't need to tell them what to do. You don't need to get angry for them or fix it for them. You just need to hear them. You just need to communicate that what they say matters to you. You just need to believe them. You don't need to tell them they are overreacting, that it's not a big deal, or that everyone in the situation is an idiot. Emotional wellness occurs when we can communicate to ourselves and others that our emotions matter and that the emotions of others matter.

Language also has a huge impact on our brains and even our bodies. Certain words have a lot of baggage attached to them, and when we think them or hear them, we can change our physiology. I learned this firsthand when I was preparing to give birth. I read a book by the midwife Ina May, and she discussed how emotional safety and language are critical for women who are in labor. One example is instead of calling a contraction a "contraction," her midwife community called it a "rush." She discussed that what you say and how you say it to a woman in labor can have a profound impact on her body and on her mind, and I know this firsthand from my own experiences.[9]

Another way that I use this myself is if I am having trouble sleeping. The word *ease* brings me calm and relief, so I breath in and think the word *ease*. I breathe out and think the word *peace*. This has a profound impact on what is called the parasympathetic nervous system, which triggers a "rest and digest" response, the opposite of a fight-or flight response.

Be intentional with the language you use, especially around children. When a child feels fully seen and acknowledged by those around him, it's hard for him not to feel loved and secure. This sense of security—what psychologists call secure attachment—is the stabilizer of a child's emotional life into middle school and adolescence and into the formation of his or her adult relationships. A child who feels free to experience the full range of emotions without fear of punishment or the need for self-censorship learns these key lessons:

Emotions pass. They are transient. There is nothing in mental experience that demands an action. Emotions are not scary. No matter how big or bad any particular feeling seems in the moment, you are bigger than it is. Emotions are teachers. They contain information that can help you figure out what matters to you and to others.[10] This does not mean that parents tolerate tantrums or irrational behavior, but it does mean that you acknowledge and accept their feelings without rebuke.

Be intentional with your nonverbals and understand that your emotional health impacts others. It is impossible to be around another human without being influenced by their emotional state. It's a concept called emotional contagion. We can all think about times when our own parents were upset and we were influenced by it, even if they didn't say a word. It's motivating for us to take care of our emotional health because we know everyone around us will benefit if we do.

Many times, our feelings don't reflect reality. Your feeling is real, but that doesn't mean it's true. If you feel like nobody cares about you or understands you, it doesn't mean that nobody cares about or understands you. Sometimes when my kids are overtired or frustrated, they will say things like, "We never do anything fun" or, "You never listen to me." It doesn't pay for me to argue with them or to prove them wrong. The most effective response is validating how they feel in the moment—"That is frustrating!" If you yourself feel like nobody ever listens to you, remind yourself that this is a feeling and it doesn't mean it is absolutely true. Ask yourself where this feeling is guiding you and use it to ask assertively for what you need. If you feel like your spouse never listens to you, you can communicate it by saying, "I'm feeling disconnected and would like to talk. Is there a good time when I can have your full attention?" Although this sounds like the response of a counselor, it is much more effective than giving feedback out of frustration.

The Bible has a lot to say about feelings. One of the primary emotions that the Bible discusses is love. It tells us that God is love (1 John 4:8). It reminds us that love binds everything together in perfect harmony (Colossians 3:14); tells us that everything we do should be done in love (1 Corinthians 16:14); and states that love bears all things, believes all things, hopes all things, endures all things (1 Corinthians 13:7). In Romans 15:13 Paul writes, **"May the God of hope fill you with all joy and peace as you trust in him, so that you may overflow with hope by the power of the Holy Spirit."** The emotions described as the fruit of the Spirit are love, joy, and peace.

The Bible says many things about the emotions of anger and anxiety. It says that we should be slow to anger and forgiving to one another. We are to cast our cares on God and not to worry about anything. This can be really challenging and hard to remember to do. Philippians 4:6,7 says, **"Do not be anxious about anything, but in every situation, by prayer and petition, with thanksgiving, present your requests to God. And the peace of God, which transcends all understanding, will guard your hearts and your minds in Christ Jesus."** We are reminded that in the world there will be trials and tribulation, but with God there is peace, hope, and joy. In John 16:33 Jesus says, **"I have told you these things, so that in me you may have peace. In this world you will have trouble. But take heart! I have overcome the world."** Isn't that so comforting to hear? Sometimes it feels like the world has overcome us and has overcome Christians. But as we know, just because it feels that way, doesn't mean it's true. It's overwhelming living in a fallen, sinful world, but as God reminds us, he has overcome the world. We can turn our frustration into fascination. The world and our brains cannot even comprehend the peace that Christ gives to us. Our logic cannot understand it because it is so powerful.

When we are feeling despair, God tells us that he is with us. Psalm 34:18 says, **"The Lord is close to the brokenhearted and saves those who are crushed in spirit."** Our spirits can feel crushed by the suffering in the world. We can feel crushed by the news. We can feel crushed by our social media feeds, but we know that we have a God of peace and love and we have access to the peace that surpasses all understanding. Thanks be to God!

CHAPTER 6

GRATITUDE AND MANAGING EXPECTATIONS

"Give thanks in all circumstances;
for this is God's will for you in Christ Jesus."
1 Thessalonians 5:18

"Gratitude is riches. Complaint is poverty"[1]
—Doris Day

My parents are awesome parents. One particular area in which they excelled and continue to excel is in the area of what I will call "birthday celebratory-ness." My birthday was the biggest deal growing up. It started with me choosing my own box of sugar cereal and not having to share it with my siblings. An entire box of sugar cereal that I wouldn't get most days of the year was a big deal; getting it for myself only was the biggest deal. The day ended with me choosing a meal to my exact liking and a cake of my choice. My parents weren't extravagant at birthdays, but they made us feel extremely special. They do the same for their grandchildren. My expectations about the specialness of my birthday was carried into my marriage. Unfortunately for my husband, he had completely different rituals surrounding birthdays.

I remember at an embarrassingly old age in my 30s waking up on my birthday and expecting to be surprised with balloons, flowers, or birthday cereal. Instead, I was bombarded with getting the kids ready for school and not being able to find my son's blue shirt for preschool. Not only did my husband have no birthday surprises; he slept in through all of it. That's right, he slept in on my birthday while I endured the chaos of getting kids ready by myself.

In a situation like that, it is easy to let the resentful and hurtful thoughts take over. It's easy to talk about the situation with someone else and have them fuel the fire: "What a jerk! How selfish! You deserve better." It's easy to let a situation like that ruin your day and for you to have a victim mindset: "I was wronged. My husband is a jerk, and I am birthday cereal-less!"

As I was driving my son to preschool, I thought about a quote I had read about turning your expectations into appreciation. I had heard this from Tony Robbins, and he said it was a life-changing mindset shift. So I thought about my expectations. I expected the royal treatment on my birthday. I expected surprises, the perfect gifts, and to be treated like a queen all day. I didn't get any of that. So as much as my sinful nature wanted to fight it, I started to think about what I appreciate about my husband. He is an amazing dad. He is the rock of our family. He is the kindest human I know. I started thinking about everything I love and appreciate about my husband, and I felt my body and brain shift completely. My heart was so full of love that I called him and started telling him everything I appreciated about him. He answered sheepishly and was surprised and suspicious of my response to him but was receptive upon hearing how genuine I was with my love for him.

My husband slept until 7:30 A.M. on my birthday; that wasn't a deal breaker for me. When I changed what I focused on, I felt the benefits of shifting from a victim mentality to a loving, forgiving person. That is my best self. That is who I want to be in my marriage. That is how I want my husband to treat me when I inevitably screw up and hurt him in our lifespan. That is what I can do out of love for Christ. I can change my expectations into appreciation, and my whole outlook changes. I can also say that later in the day I was showered with flowers and treats and gifts from my husband. He knows me and knows that's how I feel loved. It just happened in a different way than what I expected. Expectations really are a matter of frustration and resentments waiting to happen.

Managing your expectations is critical for your mental health. The definition of *expectation* is "a strong belief that something will happen or be the case in the future." Many of us have expectations about how the government should be, how our relatives should act, how our children should obey, or even how other people should drive. We even have expectations about how we should be. I once heard the quote that frustration is a matter of expectations. You expected your Disneyland vacation to be magical, but your kids fought the whole time and someone got sick and you had to go home early. You expected your boss to appreciate your work, but it was unnoticed. You expected your guests to contribute more to the holiday meal or to thank you profusely for hosting, but it didn't happen. You expect your three-year-old to obey you all the time.

If your happiness and well-being are dependent on the world and other people and even yourself behaving the way you think they should all the time, you are setting yourself up for frustration and resentment. The world doesn't work the way we think it should. The government doesn't work the way we think it should. Other people don't behave the way we think they should. Our spouses will let us down, our kids will let us down, and we will let ourselves down. I'm not saying this to be depressing. I'm saying this because it's true. We're sinful! We live in a fallen, sinful world. Our spouses get tired and distracted and don't clean up the way we think they should. Our parents give our kids tons of sugar and let them watch more than one movie in a row even though it's never a good idea. Flights get delayed; people in our lives die.

If we can stop focusing on how other people let us down by never emptying the dishwasher and instead be grateful we have a dishwasher at all, our entire outlook changes. Our mood changes, our responses change, and our neurobiology changes. It's a choice we can make, just like thinking of what I loved about my husband instead of focusing on the fact that he didn't have a birthday surprise for me first thing in the morning. When appreciation becomes a habit, our lives change.

When I was growing up, my mom was adamant that we write thank-you notes to anyone who gave us gifts. I'm talking notes by hand, several lines of thankful sentiments sent in the mail. To this day, I don't feel like a gift is truly mine until that thank-you note is written. Even now my sister calls me if she needs one more thankful sentiment. Her thank-you notes have a formula of "Dear so and so, thank you for the gift of so and so. I love you. Love, Julia." She feels that in her adulthood she should include more polite small talk in her notes, and that is where my expertise is called upon. I'm really good at polite small talk.

It's fascinating to me how much gratitude has been discussed in mainstream psychology. A thought leader in mental health, Brené Brown, calls gratitude the most healing of all emotions and the foundation of empathy and joy. In our brains, gratitude actually releases a chemical called dopamine, which is our feel-good neurotransmitter. It is the same neurochemical that is released when eating a cupcake or snorting a line of cocaine. Not only does it signal pleasure to our brains; it also signals that we should keep doing what we are doing. It is our incentive and motivation neurotransmitter. Feeling gratitude releases dopamine, and this signals our bodies that it feels good and that we want to keep doing it. As opposed to a vicious cycle, the process of the neurobiology of gratitude is called the virtuous cycle. The other fascinating thing is that it is neurobiologically impossible to feel anxiety and gratitude in our brains at the same time. It is also impossible to feel gratitude and anger in our brains at the same time. A brain filled with gratitude has no room for anger or anxiety, and that blows my mind. It is so powerful.

God knows the transformational impact of gratitude. It is an act of worship in response to God in all circumstances in our lives (1 Thessalonians 5:18), and it is the state in which God asks that we come into his presence (Psalm 95:2). He asks us to come into his presence with thanksgiving. God wants us to be around him with thankful hearts. In Colossians 2:6,7 he tells us to live our lives in Christ Jesus—rooted and built up in him, strengthened in the faith as we were taught, and overflowing with thankfulness. That's not a little thankful; that is an abundance of gratitude. God reminds us that to increase our gratitude, we should increase our generosity (2 Corinthians 9:11) and our grace (2 Corinthians 4:15). Thanksgiving has a prominence in the book of Colossians and is noted in 1:12; 3:15-17; and 4:2.

In 1 Thessalonians 5:18 it says, **"Give thanks in all circumstances; for this is God's will for you in Christ Jesus."** It doesn't say to give thanks when you get your way and life is great. It says give thanks in *all* circumstances. Philippians 4:6,7 reminds us to **"not be anxious about anything, but in every situation, by prayer and petition, with thanksgiving, present your requests to God."** Thanksgiving is a crucial part of prayer and supplication. *Supplication* is "the action of asking or begging for something earnestly or humbly" (*Oxford Languages*). God asks us to pray and request things from him with thanksgiving.

Gratitude can have a transformational impact on your outlook. When my best friend Nicki died, I experienced tremendous grief over the loss. I was so distraught by her death that I broke down crying at work and at home. As I processed my grief over my friend's death, my gratitude for my friendship with her had a tremendous healing power for me. I'm grateful I knew her. I've been forever changed because of her life and death. I'm a better mom and a better person because of her faith example and her presence as a human. My tremendous gratitude for Nicki has helped me deal with her sudden death in a way that has helped integrate my grief into my brain. I still miss my friend. I still cry about the fact that she died. But I don't feel resentment or anger, and I don't feel afraid that I too may suddenly die. I used to feel survivor's guilt; on my son's first day of kindergarten, I cried for her son that he didn't have his mom at his first day of kinder-garten. I know that grief and loss are complex, but I also know that gratitude is the most healing emotion. I'm not saying gratitude will take sad feelings away, but it offers a perspective of healing instead of hurt.

Gratitude is also most effective when it is shared. You know how when you receive really good news, you are compelled to share it? We can only feel so much by our-selves; that is why we are wired to tell other people so we can share it collectively. It is the same with gratitude. It is most effective when it is shared with others and when it is specific. If you can share with your significant other the specific things you love and appreciate about them, that goes a long way. They respond to it a lot better than you sharing their list of "areas of growth."

Whenever I did couples counseling, instead of tack-ling the most painful areas first, I helped the couples develop an appreciation practice so there could be a foundation of psychological safety as they dealt with the tough stuff. I think all of us would love more apprecia-tion. Since we can't control if others communicate their appreciation to us, we can start by communicating our appreciation to others.

Make it super specific. Be genuine and authentic and really take time to articulate what you appreciate in others. If you are in a position of leadership at work, take time to communicate specifically what you appreciate about your employees. One client whom I worked with in therapy happened to be a therapist herself, and at her clinic they started a "Gratitude Week." It's kind of like a secret Santa practice, but you share treats and small gifts and tokens of appreciation. I just love that and think it would be a great practice at any workplace.

If you can start a ritual of gratitude with your family, that is a powerful way to connect and give thanks to God. One practice that I do with my kids every night is having them say their "happy, sad, worried, and grateful" for the day. If we are going to bed late and don't have time for everyone to share all those, we slim our sharing down to our "gratefuls." If someone doesn't have a "sad" or a "worried," they don't have to share, but they must share a "grateful." Sometimes one child will say they have no "gratefuls," and it's fun to see the other kids step in and remind their brother or sister of what they have to be grateful for. They always have to find a "grateful," even if it was a hard day.

Making gratitude a habit is a helpful way to make it automatic. BJ Fogg out of Stanford developed a concept called "habit stacking," where you have one thing you do every day that triggers the development of a new habit. It's a simple, fascinating idea. The example that he used is that every time he went to the bathroom, he did one push-up. Although I'm not sure how that worked in public places, he talked about how this habit-stacking practice led him to lose 30+ pounds and now do well over one hundred push-ups a day.[2]

I loved this idea and wanted to try it on myself. Although most of my attempts didn't stick, a gratitude habit did. I remember the exact moment when I realized that this habit was automatic—I didn't have to consciously think about it. On my walk to my office at work, I would think about what I was grateful for when I saw a certain tree outside my office. I did and still do this every day, and I distinctly remember when I saw the tree and my brain automatically started going through my gratitude list without me intentionally thinking about it. It was cool! With enough practice, we can use the science of automatic thinking to our benefit. This helped me feel grounded after a busy morning of getting the kids ready and dropped off at school and going into a full email inbox of questions and concerns from students. My gratitude practice is a bridge that sustains me in the work I do.

REFLECTION BREAK

1. Think of one way you can incorporate a gratitude practice into your life.

2. Who can you share it with?

3. How can you use it with the habit-stacking idea? (i.e., how can something you already do like brushing your teeth, drinking coffee, driving to work, resting in bed, etc. trigger this practice?)

CHAPTER 7
BEHAVIOR AND HABITS

"So whether you eat or drink or whatever you do,
do it all for the glory of God."
1 Corinthians 10:31

"Our lives are fashioned by our choices.
First, we make our choices. Then our choices make us."[1]
—Anne Frank

Habits are the small choices that we make every day. All of us have different habits and behaviors about how we wake up in the morning, how we greet our families, the supplements we take, our hygiene practices, our routes to work (if we even have to leave our homes), how we cook food, how we tidy our houses, and how we connect with our loved ones. All our habits and behaviors look different. They say that habits account for about 40% of our behavior on a given day, and most habits are automatic. You don't think about them; you just do them. It's kind of like flushing the toilet. You don't make a conscious choice as to whether or not you should flush; you engage in this habit mindlessly. If you have small children, you know that flushing the toilet isn't an automatic human behavior. It has to be taught in young ones. When we want to develop a good habit or break a bad habit, it's really important that we start to develop an awareness of what we actually do.

Awareness is the first step. I started to notice that every time I changed my clothes, I threw them on the floor or on a bench in my bedroom. When the pile became a certain height, I put the clothes away. Changing clothes and throwing them on the floor became so automatic that I wasn't even aware I was doing it. I distinctly remember looking at the floor and making myself pick up my clothes immediately. I am currently teaching the same methodology to my own children. When we change, we deal with our clothes immediately, whether it is throwing them down the laundry chute or putting them away.

It's critical to understand the science of habits and use it to our advantage. Helpful habits can become automated too. If we want to direct our behavior toward our values, we transform our intentional behaviors into habits, making them so deeply ingrained that we no longer have to be intentional about them at all. Consider the values exercise you completed in chapter 3. If you haven't done this, take some time to reflect on two or three of your core values. When you have clarity in what matters to you, you can develop habits that help support the things you care about. The beauty of deliberately cultivating habits in line with our values is that they can persist over time with almost no further effort, on good days and on bad, when we're really paying attention and when we're not. No matter how frazzled we are in the morning, we always remember to brush our teeth and to fasten our seat belts as soon as we get into the car. The ability to form values-connected habits not only makes our intentions durable, it frees up our minds for other tasks as well.[2]

REFLECTION BREAK

Take some time to write out four habits that you would like to build and four you would like to stop.

Four habits I would like to build:

Four habits I would like to stop:

Some examples that I have worked on are flossing my teeth every day, drinking more water, writing thank-you notes, watching less TV, engaging in less social media, and reading every day. Habit development that is a continued evolution is moving my body every day for 30 minutes and meal planning every week.

When you want to engage in a new habit, make it pleasurable and desirable. When I think about working out, there is still an aspect of shame and pain associated with going to the gym for me. I think about myself needing to leave my warm, cozy house and running on a treadmill in too tight clothes. I think about the fit and beautiful people at the gym who will look me up and down and think about what a lost cause I am. In reality, I know this is not true, but there is still an aspect of resistance to going to the gym for me. It doesn't sound fun. I resist going because it is associated with pain and discomfort.

When I really thought about how to make the experience of going to the gym desirable for me, I made a few shifts to make it fun. Now the first thing I do when I go to our local YMCA is sit in the steam room. I live in Minnesota, and it is cold here for much of the year. Going into a warm, quiet steam room by myself is an absolute treat. I leave my house in the cold weather, drive across town, and immediately go to the steam room and get warm and cozy. That is the reward I get for going to the gym, and it has rewired my association. I usually row or go on an elliptical machine, and I turn the television channel to Home and Garden Television (HGTV). This whole ritual of going to the steam room and then watching HGTV while I work out has completely transformed how I view the gym. It has caused me to associate my time there with pleasure and relief instead of thinking about it as painful.

Whatever new habits you want to build, make them fun! If you associate a behavior with pain, you are much less likely to do it. If you associate a behavior with pleasure, the odds are you will likely engage in this behavior. The same goes for getting together with people. If you think about getting together with friends or other couples as a painful chore, you are less likely to do it. One thing my husband and I agreed upon is that if we host, we are not going to stress out about it. We tend to host quite a bit, and we save a lot of time and energy not fretting about every imperfection of our house but instead focusing on the joy of connecting with friends and loved ones. Instead of agonizing over making everything perfect, we have fun planning food and drink menus and coming up with fun games and activities.

As you consider the habits you would like to develop and those you would like to stop, think of ways you can make them pleasurable and think of how you can make those you want to stop painful.

MAKE GOOD HABITS OBVIOUS AND BAD HABITS HARD

Every time I've gone to the dentist since I've been a child, I've felt embarrassed about my lack of flossing habit. When the dental hygienist asked if I flossed, I replied, "Umm, sort of?" as my gums bled. I like to floss. I identify as a flosser. Yet it seems that in my adulthood I could never make the habit stick. It wasn't until I made flossing so easy and accessible that it was impossible not to do it. How did I do this? I bought several flossers and consistently keep one on my nightstand. Every night when I read in my bed (the book I am currently reading is also readily available on said nightstand), I floss my teeth. The last time I went to the dentist I could confidently say that I had flossed my teeth every single day. It's not that I have amazing willpower or discipline to do this; it's just that I made it super simple and removed any possible barrier.

Make good habits easy to do. Researchers have

referred to the impact that environmental defaults can have on our decision-making as choice architecture. You can set up your environment to help make good choices really easy. How you organize furniture, what you display on your shelves, the sensory experience of your space, and the availability of items all make a difference. It is important to realize that you can curate and be the architect of your choices. You can design for default. Make good habits so easy to do that you can't possibly not do them.

It's important when you are developing new habits to remove any barriers you might have. Want to eat healthier? Buy healthy food, cut it up, and put it in to-go containers or in the front of your fridge. Put the fresh fruit or the avocados out so you will easily see them and consume them. Have good books on hand, position your piano or instruments in a high traffic area in your home, or get a really great beverage container that holds water.

With all change, you have to start really small. I have a tendency to overwhelm myself. Whenever I want to eat better, I buy a ton of vegetables and throw away anything processed and then lament that we have no food and order a pizza. The vegetables sit in our veggie drawer until I find them squishy and soggy several days later. Whenever I want to work out more, I lift or run really hard until I'm too sore to go back to the gym or I see I haven't lost any weight in two solid weeks of working out. Then I quit. When I want to drink more water, I force myself to drink a gallon, and then I hate it and go back to what I always do. In all the wellness and habits literature, starting small is a huge theme. Start so small you can't fail. If you do fail, then you weren't starting small enough, and you need to go back and start even smaller. This seems really dumb at first and like you are trying to trick your brain, but in my experience, it does actually work.

Small changes that add up is a concept called the "aggregation of marginal gains." When you start making small changes, they add up to a big change. As Jim Rohn said, "Success is a few simple disciplines, practiced every day; while failure is simply a few errors in judgment, repeated every day. It is the accumulative weight of our disciplines and our judgments that leads us to either fortune or failure."[3] For a change to be sustainable, it has to be integrated into your life. You start by saving one extra dollar a month. You start by taking one deep breath. You start by having one more carrot a day or drinking one more glass of water a day. Like I said, I have the tendency to go big and then get discouraged and stop. For anything to be sustainable, start small, start where you are.

REFLECTION BREAK

1. Where can you improve your life by 1%?

2. How can you strengthen your faith by 1%?

3. How can you improve your marriage by 1%?

4. How can you improve your relationships with your children by 1%?

5. How can you improve your health by 1%?

6. How can you increase your joy by 1%?

A critical part of habits also goes back to the idea of identity. We as humans strive to operate in alignment with how we define ourselves. I define myself as a boring mom, so on weekends you can typically find me reading a book with a cup of tea and being in bed by 9:30 P.M. I don't identity as someone who is wild and crazy, and my behaviors are reflective of that. When thinking about any sort of goal you might have, don't ask yourself, "What do I want to do?" Instead ask yourself, "Who do I want to become?"

Any sustainable behavior change has to be an identity change. The goal is not to run a marathon; the goal is to become a runner. The goal is not to write one book on self-care; the goal is to become a writer. The goal is not to learn how to play one instrument; the goal is to become a musician. It's not about accomplishing a goal; it's about who you become in the process. As you continue to reflect on this, think about ways you can serve God and spread the gospel. How can you continue to develop into the person God has created you to be?

So many people have things they want to accomplish, but after they accomplish their goals, they feel a sense of emptiness or disappointment that meeting that goal didn't bring them the happiness or the satisfaction they were expecting. Many of the men who were involved in first landing on the moon became alcoholics after that historic event. What did they have to look forward to? As a Christian, you can instead focus on God's love and will for you rather than relying on accomplishing big goals to make you happy. The biggest goal that could ever be accomplished has already been finished. It was finished through Jesus' live, death, and resurrection from the dead. Because of what Jesus did for you, eternal life in heaven is yours! You can approach your goals with confidence, knowing that the battle has been won. Second Timothy 1:7 says, **"For the Spirit God gave us does not make us timid, but gives us power, love and self-discipline."** With God's help, focus on developing a spirit of power, love, and self-discipline. Remember that your goals are founded in Christ.

I remember when I completed my doctorate, I almost felt a sense of emptiness and a loss of identity after my dissertation was complete. I had spent the past four years working toward this goal, not to mention the six years of undergraduate college and my master's work. Once my dissertation was complete and I was a doctor, I felt like I had lost a part of my purpose. It wasn't the grand satisfaction and relief I was anticipating. Instead of being grateful to God and honoring him with the process, I was searching for my own fulfillment and my own glory.

I know now that it was God's process of teaching me and stretching me to lengths that I never knew were possible that was so rewarding. It didn't matter as much that I was done with my degree; it mattered that I had improved along the way. Instead of waiting to accomplish your goal to feel happy, embrace the process.

HABITS AND SYSTEMS

Once you have an idea of who you want to become, it's critical to develop a system to help get you there. In *Atomic Habits,* James Clear says, "We don't rise to the level of our goals; we fall to the level of our systems."[4] This is incredibly important when we are analyzing what we do. What is your system for making these changes sustainable? Is your system for eating dinner to see what happens around 5:00 P.M. and decide if you want fast food or something to quickly air fry? Is your system for reading a book to think, "I should find a good book" and then never really following through? Many times we have great goals that we want to achieve but no system to get us there.

I focus a lot on systems in my own life. Every time I start a new semester of teaching, I typically call my first week back my "system setting" week. I develop a plan for morning routines, getting kids to school, doing household chores and homework, keeping up with work obligations, and meal planning. I think about when I can get my workouts in. My husband and I both study and analyze what works in our systems and what doesn't work. We absolutely are not robotic about it, and many of our systems are definitely works in process. We are still working on systems for our kids putting their winter gear away consistently and for meal planning, etc. If you focus on systems instead of outcomes, the outcomes will take care of themselves.

REFLECTION BREAK

What is your system for

- improving your life by 1%?

- strengthening your faith by 1%?

- improving marriage by 1%?

- strengthening relationships with your children by 1%?

- improving your health by 1%?

- increasing your joy by 1%?

As we consider the habits that we engage in, remember that we must obey God (Acts 5:29) and act with a spirit of humility (1 Peter 5:5). God reminds us to stay away from the works of the flesh in Galatians 5:19-21 and to imitate him (Ephesians 5:1-33). He tells us to walk in love and **"to live self-controlled, upright and godly lives"** (Titus 2:12). We want our behavior to reflect the will of God because we are his workmanship, created in Christ Jesus to do good works, which God prepared beforehand for us (Ephesians 2:10). We want our behavior to reflect godly living and putting God first, and we trust in the Lord with all our hearts and lean not on our own understanding. God will make straight our paths (Proverbs 3:5,6). All our habits and behaviors are not done for our own glory but for the glory of God. John 15:8 reminds us, **"This is to my Father's glory, that you bear much fruit, showing yourselves to be my disciples."**

CHAPTER 8
PERSPECTIVE AND MEANING MAKING

"Set your mind on things above, not on earthly things."
Colossians 3:2

"We don't see the world as it is; we see it as we are."[1]
—Anais Nin[1]

One of the most powerful stories I have heard comes from a 95-year-old psychologist named Edith Eger. I heard her story in a podcast interview. Edith is an Auschwitz concentration camp survivor. When she was 16, she was getting ready to go on a date with her boyfriend, and there was a knock on the door. At the door were Nazi soldiers, and within minutes, Edith and her family were on a train to Auschwitz. Her parents were murdered immediately upon their arrival. While on the train, Edith's mother said to her, "Edith, remember that no one can take away what you put in your mind." Her first night there, she was asked to dance for the prison guards, and she remembered what her mother had said to her. She danced as if she were on a stage in Budapest. Edith lived through the atrocities of the concentration camp and was eventually rescued by an American solider when he saw her hand move under a pile of corpses. Edith eventually became a psychologist and studied the mind and human behavior, but she reflected on her experience of Auschwitz with deep forgiveness. She said, "I was not a prisoner there. In my mind, I was free. The guards were the prisoners."[2] She also made the journey to Hitler's home in Germany, specifically so she could forgive him.

Edith's story is incredibly inspiring, especially because it shows the power of our perspectives and the meanings we give to our experiences. "Meaning making" is the idea that what a situation means to us is something that we can intentionally decide.

Another Holocaust survivor, Viktor Frankl, states, "We must never forget that we may also find meaning in life even when confronted with a hopeless situation, when facing a fate that cannot be changed. For what matters is to bear witness to the uniquely human potential at its best, which is to transform a personal tragedy into a triumph, to turn one's predicament into a human achievement. When we are no longer able to change a situation, we are challenged to change ourselves.[3]

The language we use to describe ourselves and our circumstances is critical. Are you having a break *down*, or are you having a break *through*? It's truly a matter of perspective. Are you getting *punished* by God or *challenged* by God? I was recently doing a puzzle with my son Jack, and he said, "I can't do this; this is too hard." I said, "It is hard, but it's a good challenge." Jack kept doing the puzzle. The word *challenge* automatically makes you reframe the situation into something that can be overcome. You can feel the difference when you say, "I can't do this; the situation is hopeless" versus, "This is really hard, but I'm up for the challenge." I think what is important to understand is that shifting your perspective, meaning, and mindset does not deny pain or pretend that things aren't painful or hard. It's not just positive thinking, like walking out to a garden and saying, "There are no weeds, there are no weeds, there are no weeds." Thinking there are no weeds will not take the weeds out of your garden. One perspective would be to say, "There are too many weeds. I can't handle them all, and I'm going to give up" versus, "I have a lot of weeds in my garden, and I'm overwhelmed. How can I get help in taking them out?"

There is a sub facet of the wellness realm that has been deemed toxic positivity. You can picture it, because this is likely generated by someone you follow online, whether it's an acquaintance or an influencer. This is the content that says we never struggle, that everything is always perfect, and that struggle is abnormal or not welcome. The phrase "good vibes only" actually perpetuates this movement. Susan David, in her book *Emotional Agility*, talks about toxic positivity and how it can lead to despair. People who feel the whole range of emotions feel like something is wrong with them if they aren't feeling good vibes only all the time. The goal isn't to feel positive all the time or to only have "good vibes." The point is to be able to have perspective and to give your experience context.

REFRAMING YOUR SITUATION

Reappraisal or cognitive reframing strategies are a way to reimagine whatever is triggering an emotional experience and then react instead to that new inter-pretation. The basic principles of reframing are that we consciously choose to view a situation in a way that gen-erates the least negative emotion in us, or we attempt to take the perspective of the person who is activating us and assume the best intention.[4] If you wake up and say good morning to your spouse and he ignores you, instead of thinking, "What a jerk!" think instead of what could be happening that caused him to respond that way. Is he distracted? Did he hear you? Is he upset about something else? Assuming positive intent in people helps generate understanding and empathy in the situation instead of anger and resentment.

There are many studies that looked at how the meaning participants gave a concept greatly changed their outcomes. There was an experiment conducted at a large business where over the course of a week, they showed a video about stress to two groups of workers. The first group was shown a video that discussed the harmful effects of stress—bad for health, detrimental to job performance, and an obstacle to learning. The second group was shown a group of videos that contained the opposite message—stress is good for health and inspires better job performance as well as learning and growth. Participants who watched the three-minute "stress is positive" video three times a week had a significant reduction in negative health symptoms and an increase in job performance compared to those who watched the "stress is negative" video. Just having a negative or positive view of stress can shift our health outcomes in and of themselves!

Another study at Harvard found that students who were asked to think of test anxiety as beneficial performed better on exams than a control group. Another experiment found reframing anxiety as excitement was found to improve negotiating and public speaking skills. Reappraisal has been studied in fMRI measures of brain activity, and it dampens the activity in the part of your brain called the amygdala, the part of your brain that becomes activated when you experience strong emotions. It activates the lateral temporal cortical areas of the brain, which help modulate your emotional responses. Giving your experience a new meaning helps you process it in a healthier way.

The Bible has amazing perspective when it comes to mindset and meaning making. Suffering is inevitable and universal, but how we respond to suffering differs. One of my favorite examples of this is in Romans 5:3-5. The apostle Paul writes: **"Not only so, but we also glory in our sufferings, because we know that suffering produces perseverance; perseverance, character; and character, hope. And hope does not put us to shame, because God's love has been poured out into our hearts through the Holy Spirit, who has been given to us."**

When we are struggling, it's powerful to reframe our experience as helping us produce perseverance, character, and hope! This reminds me of the story of Jerry Coffee. Jerry was a pilot in the US Air Force who was shot down and captured with two fellow soldiers. He was held as a prisoner of war for seven years in one of the most notorious prison camps in Vietnam. One of his fellow soldiers ended his life by suicide in the cell in Vietnam. The other got out after seven years and spent the rest of his life institutionalized in the US. Jerry says that while captive, he assessed his situation and said to himself, "I'm going to be here a while. How do I use this?" He answered that question by praying every day and talking to God, because he had no one else to talk to. He worked out in his cell and strengthened his body. To stay mentally alert, he thought through every day of his life that he had lived thus far, and at the end of each day, he asked, "What did I learn today?" In an isolated cell in Vietnam, where he was brutally beaten and his basic needs weren't met, Lieutenant Coffee found a way to grow stronger mentally, physically, and spiritually. He is a living example of his suffering producing perseverance, character, and hope. He also got out after seven years and said it was the most powerful experience of his life and that he wouldn't trade it for anything. He wrote a book about it called *Beyond Survival*.[5]

Similarly, Nelson Mandela spent 27 years in prison after receiving a life in prison sentence after fighting against apartheid in South Africa. He missed his children growing up and spent nearly a quarter of a century behind bars. When asked about his perceptive in spending all that time in prison, his response was, "I was preparing."[6] He went on to win the Nobel Peace Prize in 1993, and in 1994 he became the first black president of South Africa.

Many people have heard of the concept of "fixed" versus "growth" mindsets. People with a fixed mindset follow an "entity" theory of self and believe important qualities such as intelligence and personality are fixed traits that cannot be changed. People with a growth mindset believe that these basic qualities are "malleable" and can be improved through learning and effort. Studies show that these beliefs have a profound effect on behavior. Children who believe their intelligence is fixed underperform in courses that they find difficult relative to those who believe they can improve their effective intelligence by working hard. After all, those who are open to change and believe they can do better and that their efforts matter have a sense of agency over their performance and rise to the challenge. So setbacks and failures don't keep them down, and they persevere, even when they're frustrated.[7]

We also know one's mindset can be developed and shifted. People who have a growth mindset and who see themselves as agents in their own lives are more open to new experiences, more willing to take risks, more persistent, and more resilient in rebounding from failure.

REFLECTION BREAK

1. What are ways that you can develop a growth mindset?

2. What situations are keeping you stuck? What patterns of interaction or what past situations are filling you with pain, anger, resentment, hatred, bitterness, and anguish? What ways can you reframe this situation? What ways can you grow from it? How can you use it to strengthen your faith? How can you glorify God with these struggles?

3. Write out a situation that is keeping you stuck and a way that you can see it helping you grow stronger.

With the reframing mentality, we have nothing to fear, not even death itself. As Paul writes in Philippians 1:21: **"To live is Christ and to die is gain."**

CHAPTER 9

CONNECTION AND COMMUNITY

*"Carry each other's burdens, and in
this way you will fulfill the law of Christ."*
Galatians 6:2

*"You can't stay in your corner of the forest waiting for others
to come to you. You have to go to them sometimes."*[1]
—A. A. Milne, Winnie the Pooh

My best friend was killed when we were 33 years old. I'll never forget when my mom called to tell me that Nicki had died. I was riding in my car with my husband and three kids on a Sunday afternoon in June. My mom called me, and I knew immediately something was wrong. She told me that my best friend and her husband had gotten into a motorcycle accident the night before. My mom was struggling to talk, and I remember feeling confused. She said, "Matt is doing okay, but Nicki didn't make it." I was in shock. My best friend was a stay-at-home mom;

she wasn't supposed to be dead from a motorcycle accident. She was riding with her husband; she was wearing a helmet. They were taking a Saturday night cruise with another couple, and a deer walked in front of them. They hit the deer, and my friend died on the scene. She had three young children—ages 1, 3, and 5, the exact same number and ages of my children. We had been pregnant together every time. She visited me in the hospital when I had my first son, and she cried while she held him, because she was pregnant with her first son at that time. I had just been to her farm for a playdate with my kids the previous week. That night, the church where she was a member hosted an outdoor event in their parking lot as a way to come together and grieve. We cried and prayed and sang together. It was at the height of COVID, and we were craving connection. It was a traumatic loss for all of us, and we needed to grieve together. That night, Nicki's pastor shared what Nicki had written in her will, which she had recently updated with her husband. This 33-year-old wrote: *"I'm in heaven with our Savior Jesus, pain free, and someday with faith in our Savior, we will meet again. Love you—Nicole."*

Nicki's death had a profound impact on me. When she died, several people called her their best friend, myself included. She was an absolute connector. She arranged and hosted gatherings with our high school friends, including our yearly treasured Cookie Jamboree, where we were supposed to make cookies around the holiday but typically ended up drinking wine and talking together. During COVID she made sure we stayed connected through group video calls, and she was so good about checking in and sending support. When she died, I grieved not only the loss of a dear friend, but it made me realize the importance of Christian friends, among other things.

Relationships are one of the most important aspects of our lives. Being part of an engaging community gives us a sense of belonging, a core need for human beings. There is an abundance of research that shows the enormous influence that relationships have on our well-being. People with strong social networks enjoy better mental and physical health and even live longer. A lack of connection to other people is associated with many unfavorable health outcomes, including addiction. Have you ever been in a place where you just wanted someone to understand what it felt like to be you? Maybe it was after a fight with a spouse, during a period of grief, during a situation that felt like no one got it, or when you felt like you couldn't share your experience with anyone else? That's what disconnection feels like. That's what isolation feels like. That's what loneliness or even hopelessness feels like.

In all the research on wellness, happiness, addiction, and mental health, one of the biggest protective factors are strong connections with other people. One of the longest longitudinal studies out of Harvard followed a cohort of men for almost 75 years, collecting thousands of pieces of data about them including their incomes, physical health information, mental health information, and the life issues they were facing. There were interviews with their spouses, children, and grandchildren. The study wanted to find out what makes a happy and meaningful life. The biggest finding of the study was that the quality of the relationships that these participants had was the biggest predictor of happiness. The quality of their marriages reported in their 50s was found to be a better predictor of health in their 80s than their blood pressure was! Relationships don't just feel good for us emotionally; they are healthy for us physically as well. [2]

Psychologists have found that we have a network in our brains that constantly scans our social world. If it detects we're not securely connected, our self-esteem plummets and our stress response is triggered. We become anxious and unhappy and are at great risk of becoming physically and mentally ill. [3] Dan Buettner, the cofounder of Blue Zones—an organization that studies regions of the world where people live the longest and healthiest lives—recognized the importance of community and its relationship to longevity. Along with diet and lifestyle practices, Buettner found that longevity was tied to several aspects of community: close relationships with family and a tribe with shared beliefs and healthy behaviors. [4]

Relationships come in many different forms. It's good to have healthy ties to our spouses, families, friends, and colleagues. It's also healthy to seek to feel connected to strangers we interact with briefly on a day-to-day basis.

A 2021 study by psychologist Paul Van Lange and Simon Columbus found that positive interactions with strangers "help us serve basic needs such as feeling connected, appreciated, along perhaps with the realization of personal growth in ourselves." They advise people to have "initial brief interactions, even a smile to strangers."[5]

A psychologist named Nicholas Epley also found the benefits of interacting with strangers in research he conducted studying the behavior of strangers on trains. He had three groups of commuters in Chicago do one of three things. Group one was told to keep to themselves, group two was asked to do what they would ordinarily do, and the third group was asked to reach out and say hello to someone and start a conversation. Prior to the experiment, he had asked the participants how they would feel if they were made to do the third option. They said they wouldn't like it and reported it would make them enjoy their commute less. They predicted that 40% of commuters would be happy to chat. The results of the study found that every single one of the strangers they reached out to was happy to connect. The connection did not ruin their commute as they anticipated it would. It made them happier, and that happiness carried over into the rest of the day.[6] We are wired for connection.

Unfortunately, the quantity and quality of our relationships as a group have been declining since the '50s. Although we are the most connected society there has ever been, we are also the loneliest. As Christians, we

CONNECTION AND COMMUNITY

need each other! One of the biggest blessings of community is realizing you are not alone. Realizing you are not alone is very healing. Even when you feel alone and misunderstood after a fight or in a particularly challenging life phase, God is with you. We have a connection with God, and we have the joy and opportunity to connect with others in the faith. What a blessing!

Jesus himself is a wonderful example of how important it is to have a group and to have support. He chose his disciples to follow him, and they played a pivotal part in his ministry and in spreading his teachings around the world. They supported each other, they encouraged one another, and they challenged each other.

It is critical to choose your friends wisely. God consistently reminds us to stay in unity with fellow believers and to watch for division. He urges us to create friendships with believers of good character. First Corinthians 15:33 reminds us: **"Do not be misled. 'Bad company corrupts good character.'"** Proverbs also warns of the destruction that bad friendships may bring about. Proverbs 18:24 says, **"One who has unreliable friends soon comes to ruin, but there is a friend who sticks closer than a brother."** And Proverbs 22:24,25 also reminds us of how we can be influenced by those we spend time with. It says, **"Do not make friends with a hot-tempered person, do not associate with one easily angered, or you may learn their ways and get yourself ensnared."** Proverbs even says that the righteous choose their friends carefully, but the way of the wicked leads them astray (12:26). We become who we hang out with. James 4:4 makes an analogy of the danger of becoming friends with the world that could lead to enmity against God. It says, **"Anyone who chooses to be a friend of the world becomes an enemy of God."**

God desires for us to love and serve one another. In 1 Peter 4:8 he says, **"Above all, love each other deeply, because love covers over a multitude of sins,"** and in John 15:12,13 he says, **"My command is this: Love each other as I have loved you. Greater love has no one than this: to lay down one's life for one's friends."** God also calls us to serve one another. First Peter 4:10 says, **"Each of you should use whatever gift you have received to serve others, as faithful stewards of God's grace in its various forms."**

REFLECTION BREAK

1. What are ways that you can deepen your friendships?

2. What are ways that you can deepen your Christian community?

I often think about my grandparents on both sides of the family and the fabulous communities they cultivated when they were young parents in the 1950s and 1960s. They were friends with the people they worked with and their neighbors. They had card nights, dinner parties, and went on vacation together. My parents also did a great job of connecting with friends and their siblings.

The sense of community in our country has declined significantly since the 1960s. The number of close friends people report having has also steadily declined since that time. The breaking up of nuclear families and the rise of technology disconnects us from our elders and our communities.

COVID exacerbated this disconnection, and we are still feeling the effects of it. I made it a priority for our family to develop a stronger community of friendship in our church. My husband and I talked and committed to opening our home to hosting. We agreed that we wouldn't stress when we have gatherings at our house; we want to be a place where people feel welcome and comfortable. We have a big house that we are renovating. Our house isn't perfect, and people feel comfortable that it isn't a model home.

I started my goal of community by hosting a 1920s themed dinner party for some couples from church. We started having pizza nights with grilled pizzas and expanded into game nights and movie nights for the kids. This started a weekly playdate. Our church started connect groups, where people can gather together outside of church and have a Bible study and fellowship. We hosted a connect group series in our home, and I think we had around 45 people at the first one! Now we have a robust community and feel connected to the other families at our church.

Other families began to host couples' nights and game nights and other events from Oktoberfest to an Olympics-themed summer party. This has been an incredible protective factor for us. Other people know our kids. We know other people's kids. We have similar values about our faith along with our health, parenting, marriage, etc. We have been with each other through miscarriages, financial struggles, kid issues, and parents' divorces. We have built a support system that stemmed from the death of my friend.

Building a support system takes effort and getting out of your comfort zone. It can be awkward and uncertain to get to know a new person or a new family. It takes a lot of courage and vulnerability to open your home and share your life with someone. It requires the possibility of rejection. You may invite someone to an event at your house, and they might not want to go. It can be awkward not knowing what to expect if you don't know someone well. People inevitably cancel at the last minute due to childcare issues or sick kids. It's part of life. Don't miss out on connections because you don't feel like you're rich enough, stylish enough, or have your house or your home together.

If you don't have people over because you don't think your house is nice enough or you don't think you are interesting enough or it just seems like too much work, I urge you to reconsider. Come up with a way to build community that feels manageable and good to you. If you don't want to host, consider meeting at a park with someone you want to deepen a relationship with. I'm sure there is someone in your life you want to get to know better, and I challenge you to initiate a connection attempt.

It's also extremely good for your marriage to do new things together and to get out of your comfort zone. No good story ever started with . . . remember that time we were watching Netflix together for the sixth time that week? We need to get off our couches, away from our screens, and back into our tribes. It's easier not to initiate connecting with others, and it's easier to defer to our phones or watching a new TV series. But long term, it's fun and fulfilling to cultivate relationships with others, especially those who share our faith.

It takes social risk, a little work, and some discomfort. When you feel that discomfort, know that it isn't bad. It may not be comfortable, but typically great things aren't created in your comfort zone, and relationships are included in that. I'm not saying you have to host a Met Gala, but create more intention around building a tribe.

The Bible has numerous examples of connection and community. Elisha offered his support and fellowship to the prophet Elijah. Second Kings 2:2 demonstrates Elisha's faithfulness. It says, **"Elijah said to Elisha, 'Stay here; the Lord has sent me to Bethel.' But Elisha said, 'As surely as the Lord lives and as you live, I will not leave you.' So, they went down to Bethel."** Friendship and community offer support and encouragement for us, and we are also commanded to support one another. First Thessalonians 5:11 says, **"Therefore encourage one another and build each other up, just as in fact you are doing."** Ecclesiastes 4:10 says, **"If either of them falls down, one can help the other up. But pity anyone who falls and has no one to help them up."**

It is a joyful thing to have a community in Christ. Psalm 133:1 describes this beautiful feeling of unity. It says, **"How good and pleasant it is when God's people live together in unity!"** Romans 12:10 says to **"be devoted to one another in love. Honor one another above yourselves."** In Romans 12:16 Paul goes on to say, **"Live** in harmony with one another. Do not be proud, but be willing to associate with people of low position." Paul also describes the church with a metaphor of a body. He discusses that there are many parts to the body and all the parts are needed. He says in 1 Corinthians 12:27: "Now you are the body of Christ, and each one of you is a part of it." In verses 24 and 25 he says, "God has put the body together . . . so that there should be no division in the body, but that its parts should have equal concern for each other. If one part suffers, every part suffers with it; if one part is honored, every part rejoices with it." Focus on building your tribe with intentionality.

It is critically important for your wellness to have a support system and a community where you feel like you belong. Connecting with others increases happiness. Participating in a community bonded by attitudes, values, and goals is an essential ingredient to enjoying a fulfilling life.

Choose your support system wisely. Start to develop relationships with others in your church and connect through your shared faith in Christ. Love each other in your community as Christ has loved you.

CHAPTER 10

CLOSING AND FINAL THOUGHTS

I hope this book will be a blessing to you. Here is a recap of what was discussed, with further prompts for deeper reflection. God's blessings as you continue your wellness journey!

CHAPTER 2:
WHAT IS SELF-CARE, AND WHY DOES IT MATTER?

Self-care is behavior people engage in to promote their good health and well-being. Self-care helps you nourish your body, mind, and faith. Self-care is not selfish, and it is not rationalizing nonproductive behavior. Engaging in self-care helps you support others more effectively and fully. It helps you serve God and others with your best self.

What were previous beliefs you held about self-care?

How did this chapter change these beliefs?

Why is self-care important to you?

What does God say about self-care?

CHAPTER 3:
WHO AM I? THE ROLE OF IDENTITY IN WELLNESS

Identity is a critical indicator of your behavior. Understanding your identity is important to clarifying who you are and who you want to become. God sees you in Christ's image, and this is the most beautiful and perfect identity you can have—God's own child!

What identities did you develop as a child based on the feedback you received?

What labels do you attach to yourself now?

What are your core values?

Why is understanding your core values important?

What does alignment look like to you?

CHAPTER 4:
THE MIND

The mind and brain are separate entities, and our brains change based on our experiences. We think between 60,000 and 90,000 thoughts per day, and oftentimes our thoughts are not true. What we focus on shapes our experiences powerfully, and God commands us to focus on excellent things.

What is a pattern of focus that creates distress and suffering for you?

How can you use the information in this chapter to shift your focus?

What are things you can focus on that fit with the adjectives mentioned in Philippians 4:8 (*true, noble, right, pure, lovely, admirable, excellent,* or *praiseworthy*)?

How can you encourage those around you to think of things that fit under the categories mentioned in Philippians 4:8?

CHAPTER 5:
EMOTIONS

Emotions have long been discounted in our society but serve as important information for us. They don't need to be fixed, suppressed, numbed, or discounted. It is important to view your emotions with curiosity, label them effectively, and share them with others. When others share their emotions with you, listening to them is a gift you can give them. You don't need to fix their experience or try to make it better. You can just believe them and reflect back what they are feeling. You can sit and cry with them. You know that God is a God of love and offers you the peace that surpasses all understanding. You know that you need not be anxious in anything and you can be slow to anger. You know that God is a God of hope and he will fill you with joy and peace as you trust in him.

What are common emotions that you feel?

What messages have you received about your emotions in the past? From yourself? From others?

What messages have you given others about their emotions?

How do you feel when others tell you about their struggles? How do you respond?

What are ways you can foster more empathy?

With whom can you share your emotions?

How does the Bible help you understand emotions more fully?

CHAPTER 6:
GRATITUDE AND MANAGING EXPECTATIONS

Gratitude is the most healing emotion. From an emotional standpoint, it is the foundation of empathy and joy. It is impossible to feel anger or anxiety and gratitude in your brain at the same time. Gratitude releases the neurotransmitter dopamine into your brain, which makes you want to continue to feel it. Gratitude is most effective when it is shared.

The Bible tells us to give thanks in all circumstances to the Lord. Turning expectations into appreciation is a great way to reduce your frustration and resentment. Always expecting others, yourself, and the world to be exactly how you think they should be is a recipe for suffering. Focusing on what you have instead of what is missing is a great way to cultivate an attitude of appreciation.

What did this chapter teach you about appreciation?

What expectations do you have for yourself, others, or the world that create a pattern of frustration for you?

How can you change your expectations into appreciation?

What are ways you can remember to give thanks to God in all circumstances?

CHAPTER 7:
BEHAVIOR AND HABITS

Habits are the tiny behaviors we engage in every day. About 40% of our behaviors on a given day are habits. When you want to change a behavior, think about whom you want to become instead of the goal you want to accomplish. Focusing on the process of changing into the best person God has made you to be is more important than focusing on a single goal you can accomplish. It is helpful to go back to clarifying your values when you are thinking about the habits you would like to develop. This will help you operate in alignment, which is when your inner values match your outer actions.

You will have an easier time developing good habits when you make them easy and obvious. You will have an easier time breaking bad habits when you make them undesir-

CLOSING AND FINAL THOUGHTS

able and hard. Make sure you develop a system instead of just goals. Systems help make the process sustainable. Also be sure to start so small that you can't fail. If you fail, you started too big. Keep in mind that you want your habits and routines to be God-pleasing. God wants your behaviors to be self-controlled, upright, disciplined, and godly. You want your actions to show your faith and to do all things with love.

What did the habits chapter make you think about?

In which area of your life do you have the best habits (spiritual, physical, mental, emotional, social)?

How can you continue to build off these strengths?

In which area of your life do you need the most improvement (spiritual, physical, mental, emotional, social)?

How can your habits reflect Christ's love?

CHAPTER 8:
PERSPECTIVE AND MEANING MAKING

Your perspectives shape what things mean to you. You can create the meanings you give to your experiences. This is an important factor in resiliency and in a growth mindset. God tells you to rejoice in suffering and to know that his grace is sufficient for you. You know that you will suffer in this life, but you can view those struggles as situations to rejoice over. Doing that is relieving and empowering. It is critical to use language that helps you remember that you are learning, growing, improving, and being shaped by the hard things in life. Struggles can be your greatest teachers, and they bring you back to your heavenly Father.

What is a hard situation that you have dealt with in your life?

What did it teach you?

How can you use it? How have you used it?

How can this trial bring you closer to God?

How can this trial help you grow?

CHAPTER 9:
CONNECTION AND COMMUNITY

Some of the biggest predictors of our health and hap-piness are our social relationships. We as humans are built to connect with others. We long to be in a tribe, and we thrive when we work together. Our tribes have dis-banded before and after COVID, and it is critical that we bring them back. Building friendships and community centered around a common faith in Christ is critical at an individual, familial, and community level.

What are ways you can develop new friendships?

What are ways you can deepen existing friendships?

What are ways your church can create a stronger sense of community?

What is a fun way that you would like to start connecting with others?

Why does it matter if your relationships are strong?

Why does it matter if your Christian community is strong?

How does engaging in self-care help you better serve your community?

NOTES

CHAPTER 2

1. Eleanor Brownn's website page, accessed March 3, 2023, http://www.eleanorbrownn.com/.

2. "Self-Care Interventions for Health: What Is Self-Care?," World Health Organization, June 30, 2022, https://www.who.int/news-room/fact-sheets/detail/self-care-health-interventions#:~:text=WHO's%20definition%20of%20self%2Dcare,support%20of%20a%20health%20worker.

3. Jason Mills, Timothy Wand, and Jennifer A. Fraser, "Exploring the Meaning and Practice of Self-Care Among Palliative Care Nurses and Doctors: A Qualitative Study," *BMC Palliative Care*, April 18, 2018, National Library of Medicine, https://www.ncbi.nlm.nih.gov/pmc/articles/PMC5907186/.

4. Moira Lawler, "What Is Self-Care, and Why Is It So Important for Your Health?," *Everyday Health*, May 19, 2021, https://www.everydayhealth.com/self-care/.

CHAPTER 3

1. Edmann Neumeister, "God's Own Child, I Gladly Say It"; text is public domain.

2. Dr. Seuss, *Happy Birthday to You!* (New York: HarperCollins, 1957, 1982), 11.

CHAPTER 4

1. Eckhart Tolle, *The Power of Now: A Guide to Spiritual Enlightenment* (Mumbai, India: Yogi Impressions Books, 2006).

2. "About Mental Health: What Is Mental Health?," Centers for Disease Control and Prevention, accessed March 1, 2023, https://www.cdc.gov/mentalhealth /learn/index.htm#:~:text=Mental%20health %20includes%20our%20emotional,others%2C%20and %20make%20healthy%20choices.&text=Mental %20health%20is%20important%20at,childhood %20and%20adolescence%20through%20adulthood.

3. "Depression (Major Depressive Disorder)," Mayo Clinic, accessed March 22, 2023, https://www .mayoclinic.org/diseases-conditions/depression /symptoms-causes/syc-20356007.

4. Renee D. Goodwin, Lisa C. Dierker, Melody Wu, Sandro Galea, Christina W. Hoven, and Andrea H. Weinberger, "Trends in U.S. Depression Prevalence From 2015 to 2020: The Widening Treatment Gap," *American Journal of Preventive Medicine*, September 19, 2022, https://www.ajpmonline.org/article /S0749-3797(22)00333-6/fulltext.

5. "What Is Irritable Male Syndrome (IMS)?," BodyLogicMD, accessed March 22, 2023, https://www.bodylogicmd.com /for-men/irritable-men-syndrome/.

6. Dr. Edith Eva Eger, *The Choice: Embrace the Possible* (New York: Scribner, 2018), 7.

7. Daniel Amen, "Thoughts," *BrainMD Life*, February 26, 2015, https://brainmd.com/blog/4-questions -to-transform-your-thinking-and-lift-your-mood/.

CHAPTER 5

1. Fred Rogers, *The World According to Mister Rogers: Important Things to Remember* (New York: Hachette Books, 2003), 166.

2. Marc Brackett, *Permission to Feel: Unlocking the Power of Emotions to Help Our Kids, Ourselves, and Our Society Thrive* (New York: Celadon Books, 2019), 23.

3. C. S. Lewis, *The Problem of Pain* (New York: HarperCollins, 1996), 73.

4. Peter Salovey and John D. Mayer, "Emotional Intelligence," SAGE Journals, March 1, 1990, "https://journals.sagepub.com/doi/10.2190 /DUGG-P24E-52WK-6CDG.

5. Susan David, *Emotional Agility: Get Unstuck, Embrace Change, and Thrive in Work and Life* (New York: Penguin Random House, 2016), 180.

6. Ibid., 5.

7. Viktor Frankl, *Man's Search for Meaning* (Boston: Beacon Press, 1959), 105.

8. Rogers, *The World According to Mister Rogers*, 58.

9. Ina May Gaskin, *Ina May's Guide to Childbirth* (New York: Bantam Books, 2003), 152.

10. David, *Emotional Agility*, 227.

CHAPTER 6

1. "Doris Day: Biography," IMDb, accessed March 22, 2023, https://www.imdb.com/name/nm0000013/bio?ref_=nm_dyk_qt_sm#quotes.

2. BJ Fogg, *Tiny Habits: The Small Changes That Change Everything* (Eugene, Oregon: Harvest, 2021).

CHAPTER 7

1. Anne Frank, *The Diary of a Young Girl* (New York: Bantam Books, 1994).

2. David, *Emotional Agility*, 153.

3. Jim Rohn, *The Art of Exceptional Living* (Shippensburg, Pennsylvania: Sound Wisdom, 2022).

4. James Clear, *Atomic Habits: An Easy & Proven Way to Build Good Habits & Break Bad Ones* (New York: Avery, 2018), 27.

CHAPTER 8

1. Anais Nin, *Seduction of the Minotaur* (Athens, Ohio: Swallow Press, 1961).

2. Eger, *The Choice*, 37.

3. Frankl, *Man's Search for Meaning*, 135.

4. Brackett, *Permission to Feel*, 153.

5. Gerald Coffee, *Beyond Survival: Building on the Hard Times—A POW's Inspiring Story* (New York: Putnam's Sons, 1990).

6. Nelson Mandela, *The Prison Letters of Nelson Mandela* (New York: Liveright Publishing, 2018).

7. David, *Emotional Agility*, 227.

CHAPTER 9

1. A. A. Milne, *Winnie the Pooh* (New York: Classics Made Easy, 2022), 38.

2. Harvard Second Generation Study, accessed March 22, 2023, https://www.adultdevelopmentstudy.org/.

3. Dr. Rangan Chatterjee, *Happy Mind, Happy Life: The New Science of Mental Well-Being* (Dallas: BenBella Books, 2022), 137.

4. Dan Buettner, *The Blue Zones: 9 Lessons for Living Longer From the People Who've Lived the Longest* (Washington D.C.: National Geographic, 2012), 172.

5. Paul A. M. Van Lange and Simon Columbus, "Vitamin S: Why Is Social Contact, Even With Strangers, So Important to Well-Being?," SAGE Journals, May 27, 2021, https://journals.sagepub.com/doi/full/10.1177/09637214211002538.

6. Nicholas Epley and Juliana Schroeder, "Mistakenly Seeking Solitude," *Journal of Experimental Psychology*, October 2014, https://psycnet.apa.org/buy/2014-28833-001.

ABOUT THE WRITER

Dr. Jennifer Londgren is the program coordinator for the alcohol and drug studies program at Minnesota State University-Mankato. She is a licensed marriage and family therapist, a nationally certified counselor, and a board certified telemental health provider. Dr. Londgren's mission is supporting those who serve others, and she frequently presents to educators and mental health providers on topics related to wellness, self-care, resiliency, and innovative-teaching strategies. Jennifer is married to Trevor and has four children: Jack, Kate, Anna, and Henry.

ABOUT TIME OF GRACE

Time of Grace is an independent, donor-funded ministry that connects people to God's grace—his love, glory, and power—so they realize the temporary things of life don't satisfy. What brings satisfaction is knowing that because Jesus lived, died, and rose for all of us, we have access to the eternal God—right now and forever.

To discover more, please visit timeofgrace.org or call 800.661.3311.

HELP SHARE GOD'S MESSAGE OF GRACE!

Every gift you give helps Time of Grace reach people around the world with the good news of Jesus. Your generosity and prayer support take the gospel of grace to others through our ministry outreach and help them experience a satisfied life as they see God all around them.

**Give today at timeofgrace.org/give
or by calling 800.661.3311.**

Thank you!